Paul, Luther, and the Law

Paul, Luther, and the Law

How, Then, Shall We Live?

Perry Toso

WIPF & STOCK · Eugene, Oregon

PAUL, LUTHER, AND THE LAW
How, Then, Shall We Live?

Copyright © 2026 Perry Toso. All rights reserved. Except for brief quotations in critical publications or reviews, no part of this book may be reproduced in any manner without prior written permission from the publisher. Write: Permissions, Wipf and Stock Publishers, 199 W. 8th Ave., Suite 3, Eugene, OR 97401.

Wipf & Stock
An Imprint of Wipf and Stock Publishers
199 W. 8th Ave., Suite 3
Eugene, OR 97401

www.wipfandstock.com

PAPERBACK ISBN: 979-8-3852-5557-3
HARDCOVER ISBN: 979-8-3852-5558-0
EBOOK ISBN: 979-8-3852-5559-7

VERSION NUMBER 01/19/26

Scripture quotations are from the ESV® Bible (The Holy Bible, English Standard Version®), © 2008 by Crossway, a publishing ministry of Good News Publishers. The ESV text may not be quoted in any publication made available to the public by a Creative Commons license. The ESV may not be translated in whole or in part into any other language. Used by permission. All rights reserved.

This book is dedicated to all the saints
who, by their love, led me to the One
whose promise will take me Home.

Contents

Abbreviations | ix

Introduction | 1
Chapter 1: The Heart of the Matter | 3
Chapter 2: Pietism and the Third Use of the Law | 12
Chapter 3: Melanchthon's Third Use of the Law | 21
Chapter 4: Objections by Pietists to Defend Their Claim That the Law Is Needed to Provide Structure and Guidance for Christian Ethics | 27
Chapter 5: The Foundation for Paul's Argument Regarding the Law | 41
Chapter 6: The Third Use of the Law in the Light of Good Friday and Easter | 58
Chapter 7: Five Case Studies Demonstrating the Viability of Paul's Law-Free Ethics | 62
Chapter 8: Luther's Vocabulary Regarding the Law | 73
Chapter 9: Allure and the Necessity of Threat | 103
Chapter 10: Justifying God | 113
Chapter 11: Ethics Renewed: Freed to Resist | 117

Appendix I: VI. The Third Use of the Law | 125
Appendix II: The Heidelberg Disputation: The New Reformation Theology in Twenty-Eight Articles | 131
Bibliography | 135

Abbreviations

BAGD   Bauer, Walter, William F. Arndt, F. Wilbur Gingrich, and Frederick W. Danker. *Greek-English Lexicon of the New Testament and Other Early Christian Literature*. 2nd ed. Chicago: University of Chicago Press, 1979

LW   *Luther's Works*. Edited by Jaroslav Pelikan and Helmut T. Lehman. 55 vols. Philadelphia: Fortress, 1955–1986

WA   *Martin Luther's Werke: kritische Gesamtausgabe*. 136 vols. Weimar: Hermann Böhlau, 1883–2009

Introduction

The sure confidence and the precious assurance that one is loved by Jesus are only won through to in mortal combat. You, yourself, are the battleground between the unending accusation of the evil one versus the God-given word of promise. We hang upon a word, and nothing else at all. How that assurance arrives from this struggle is the issue underlying every subsequent page of this book.

As a missionary child who grew up in Madagascar, I was surrounded by Norwegian Lutherans who came from the upper Midwest prairies of the United States. I was, therefore, marinated in Pietism. However, my father, who turned out to be a formidable Luther champion, was decidedly no Pietist.

Strangely, there were among this missionary group Pietists who were even more pious than the others. They even had their own hilltop houses separated from the rest of us. This group called themselves The Lutheran Free Church. My father found this designation almost comically ironic.

Through the decades of missionary work, the competing theologies of my Lutheran father and the prevailing Pietism was never ending. He served his final years of mission work as seminary professor in Madagascar, chosen for that important position instead of a Pietist competing for the same nomination, who had done doctoral work at the University of Chicago. This resulted in no little acrimony between our two families. Hilariously, God saw fit to join not one but two of my brothers in holy matrimony to the daughters of that family. So we were reconciled. (Sort of.)

I write this by way of introduction to this book because I *lived* Pietism, among very pious people, and I have experienced its dangers. This book attempts to fill out the differences between how the Law is used in Paul and Luther, and how that contrasts to how the Law is used by Pietism. Hopefully, the presented contrast will convince you more strongly that:

God love *sinners*.

You qualify! "For freedom, Christ has set us free" (Gal 5:1).

Chapter 1

The Heart of the Matter

Thus says the LORD God, "Behold, I am the one who has laid as a foundation in Zion, a stone, a tested stone, a precious cornerstone, of a sure foundation."

Isaiah 28:16

The Heart of the Matter

ONE COULD MAKE A strong case that, as a Christian, our entire journey of faith consists of training for the very last minute of our life. It is in that moment where a person learns whether their assurance of salvation is based upon their faith or upon the One who is faithful. Charles Haddon Spurgeon, a Baptist called the Prince of Preachers, in one of his sermons on Gal 5 proclaimed,

> When a Christian views his evidences from the top of Sinai, he grows alarmed about his salvation . . . [but] suppose he had considered the object of his faith instead of his faith, then he would have said, "There is no failure in Him, and therefore I am safe."[1]

> It is God's remembering me that is the ground of my safety; it is not my laying hold of His covenant, but His covenant's laying hold on me. . . . The hinge of our safety is God's remembering us, not our remembering Him. Hence the covenant is an everlasting covenant.[2]

To say the same thing in a different way, a valid funeral sermon confronts the only essential question among the gathered friends and family,

---

1. Spurgeon, *Morning and Evening*, September 6.
2. Spurgeon, *Morning and Evening*, August 13.

which is, "Did he or she 'make it,' and if so, what is your warrant for asserting and preaching that claim?"

The proper foundation for Christian assurance is arguably what defined the entire program of Luther's Reformation effort. This pastoral concern inhabits all of his writings and sermons, most critically in his proudest achievement, *The Bondage of the Will*. To secure that foundation, proper authority had to be established. That meant that neither the church nor any other magisterium was allowed to claim that such things as tradition or papal proclamations or even church councils could hold equal authority to the word of God. Instead of this, Luther located narrowly, once again, the authority for Christian assurance in five *solas*: grace alone, faith alone, Christ alone, the cross alone, and the word alone (*sola gratia, sola fide, solus Christus, sola crux, sola Scriptura*).

Since logically there can be only one *sola*, each of these five are facets of one single thing: that which belongs to God alone, and that which only God himself can accomplish. Each of these *solas* direct our attention to the gospel promise that Jesus's work and Jesus's righteousness alone are the bedrock for our faith. So God alone, without any cooperation from us, is the proclaimed agent and completer of our salvation. Without that, all possibility of assurance vanishes.

How then shall we live? That is the urgent question to those under constant accusation of the Law. The Law is categorical or nothing. Human righteousness via the Law is always partial and therefore the Law can never rescue or save us from perishing forever. Since that is so, our righteousness is required to be external to us, residing in another. This new righteousness is not a cooperation! It is complete, in heaven, and unassailable by our accuser. So proper assurance is, first, properly rooted in locating and believing in the correct agency of our assurance—God's preached word of promise. The many divisions of those who call themselves Evangelical Christians seem to get this part pretty much in approximate agreement.

The celebrated *solas* of Lutheran theology are too seldom recognized for their most vital purpose in Luther's writings. These *solas* locate the proper foundation for any Christian assurance of salvation by preventing any possible conception of cooperation in that miraculous work of God. God's salvation must be by him alone, because if it in any way relies upon our cooperation, there will always be questions regarding whether my commitment to God was warmhearted enough. If not, more altar calls may be in order, so that my commitment level will be buttressed in my fearful conscience. However, if God alone is the agent, then he is faithful and, in the words of the apostle Paul, "I am sure that he who began the good work in you will carry it on to completion until the day of Jesus Christ" (Phil 1:6).

The Proper Role of the Law

This first function of the *solas* has been fulsomely covered in countless theological writings on Luther's theology. However, the second, and more vital, purpose of the *solas* has been almost completely ignored. That purpose is to attack the notion that there is any place or function of the Law in the renewed ethical walk of a Christian. This is the thesis and argument of this entire book. Unfortunately, this thesis is upheld almost uniquely by only one Christian denomination—the Lutherans—and only partially among them! Worse, it is the Lutherans themselves who birthed the branch of its believers, called Pietists, who betray both Paul's theology, and Luther's, most articulately.

The establishment of proper Christian assurance has always faced, and continues urgently to face, an even thornier problem than maintaining God's sole agency in our salvation. The issue in contention is the correct understanding of the biblical, gospel role of the Law in the life of a Christian.

Controversy soon arose over this very concern among early Reformation preachers. The winning party in this controversy betrayed Luther's central bulwark for proper Christian assurance by creating something called Article VI of the Lutheran Formula of Concord. Inserted after Luther's death, and contrary to Luther's teaching, this article gives the Law an authority and function not based upon Scripture. It maintains, against both Paul and Luther, that there are three "uses" of the Law.

But this article did not solve the controversy regarding the role of the Law in the life of a Christian. It worsened it. It introduced a five-hundred-year-long debate among Lutherans, continuing to this very day, over the question of whether there are only two uses of the Law or three.

The first side (and the position of this book) maintains that there are only two uses of the Law found in Luther's writings:

- The first use is the *civil use*, to maintain societal order (Rom 13:1). For this we have police, judges, highway patrol, teachers, parents, armed forces, and prisons.

- The second use is the *theological use*, to drive us to Christ.

The other side maintains that there is also a third use, which is that the Law is, in our journey of sanctification, a *Christian's guide* to direct us in our ethical behavior, or *walk* (which is the apostle Paul's word comprehending all of Christian ethics).

The concisely stated position on the third-use-of-the-Law side goes like this: The incentive power of the gospel and *the criterion of the Law* are operative in sanctification.

But this is the most concise definition of Pietism possible! "The criterion of the Law" is theological-speak for claiming that the Law must function to determine righteousness. But this "criterion" is assuredly found nowhere in Paul's writings. In fact, it is scorned with opprobrium and blame everywhere in his writings, nowhere more critically than in Gal 2:21: "If righteousness were through the law, Christ died to no effect." And again in Gal 1:8: "But even if we or an angel from heaven should preach to you a gospel contrary to the one we preached to you, let him be accursed." And, contrary to third-users claims, using the Law to ethically guide a Christian is found nowhere in Luther's writings either. Defending their false claim, they claim that it is "implicit" in Luther's writings.

Pietism is differentiated from Luther's theology because it agrees essentially with this divergent claim that there needs to be a third use of the Law in the Christian life. The Pietist theological position is articulated in its most complete form in Article VI of the Formula of Concord, which is included in appendix I of this book.

In complete opposition to Article VI, appendix II contains Luther's opposing theological position. It is made up of Luther's twenty-eight theses of the 1518 Heidelberg Disputation. This disputation was carefully crafted by Luther to define for his Augustinian brother monks, in a comprehensive way, the new theology that he was proposing to the Catholic Church. It would be difficult to find a more condensed form of the theology Luther held until the very end of his life. One can see from the opening group of theses how impossible it is to ascribe to Luther what by the Pietist is called the "Third Use of the Law." To cite just the first two debate theses by Luther (see appendix II):

1) The law of God, the most salutary doctrine of life, cannot advance man on his way to righteousness, but rather hinders him.

2) Much less can human works, which are done over and over again with the aid of natural precepts, so to speak, lead to that end.

We are faced with an either/or claim to truth. Either Article VI of the Formula of Concord is true or Luther's claims are true. Both cannot be true. Each claim annihilates the other.

The Minority View

The shocking thing about Pietism is that virtually every Christian denomination agrees with the position that the Law's function is to act as guide in the sanctification process of a renewed Christian's life. These denominations include, but are not limited to, Catholics, Calvinists, Methodists, Anglicans, Baptists, and all non-denominational American churches. Conservative Judaism is only slightly more emphatic regarding the Law's essence as a guide for ethics!

The Pharisees (very kindred to current Pietists) come the Jesus in John 6 with their question, "What must we do to do the works God requires?" (v. 28). Their major presupposition is that the Law's non-negotiable function is to create righteousness. Jesus, in verse 29 of that chapter, corrects their question together with their major presupposition three ways:

- This is the *work* (singular, not plural, and therefore not Law-based),
- *of God* (new agent, not them),
- that you *believe* him whom God has sent (faith versus human works).

Therefore faith, not Law, is the operative ethical power. Both Paul and Luther emphatically agree. The book of Genesis makes the same point when we hear that "Abram *believed* God and it was reckoned to him as righteousness" (Gen 15:6; italics added). If righteousness was to be reckoned to Abram on the basis of works, he had plenty of works to answer for, before righteousness was possible, such as:

- Taking Lot along, in spite of God commanding that he "go from his kindred and his father's house" (Gen 12:1),
- giving Lot his choice of the promised land, which was not his to give away (Gen 13:9),

- telling Pharaoh that Sarai was his sister (Gen 12:11–19), and
- deciding to help God along by using Hagar to conceive a son who was not of the promise (Gen 16).

Thankfully God mercifully judges none of these works, but rather recognizes Abraham's faith, clearly demonstrated in being willing to sacrifice Isaac (Gen 22).

It is nothing less than astonishing that both the apostle Paul and Luther should be so widely and completely misread! They fervently, heatedly, and comprehensively throughout their writings emphatically deny any guiding function for the Law! It is catastrophic for proper Christian assurance that the proper teaching of Paul and Luther holds such current miniscule minority status. The almost unheard Pauline and Lutheran position, that the Law has no place in guiding the new Christian's behavior, makes their actual position easy to shout down and ignore with impunity.

Critically, the Pietist insists that God's new creation, the person who has died with Christ and is raised again with him, and who is inhabited by the Holy Spirit, still needs the direction of the Law. Paul addresses this attack on his gospel in Rom 6, 7, and 8, and in the entire book of Galatians. Proper Lutherans address this attack by demonstrating that the second use of the Law, which drives us to Christ, makes the third use unnecessary. Since, in Luther's formulation, Christians remain simultaneously 100 percent sinner as well as 100 percent righteous, the Law's original function to reveal our sin is still necessary for them. But since we have already been delivered by dying with Christ in baptism, we welcome our continued execution by the Law, so that Christ may arise more fully in us. Christians cry to the Law, "Come and kill me! I want to be more like Christ!" No other human being, other than a Christian, could dream of saying the same thing.

Pietists' fear-driven misunderstanding of the Law's function produces claims, which posit falsely, that there exists only the following alternatives. They say that if the guidance of the Law is absent from Christian ethics, then what inevitably happens is that one becomes one or all of these:

- An antinomian, one who believes he is released by grace from any obligation to observe the Law,
- an anarchist, one who ignores all authority or Law, or

- a gospel reductionist, a person who believes that since one is justified by grace, you can simply relax and need to do nothing.

You will find the attack upon Paul's gospel, from this side, refuted in his First Letter to the Corinthians.

Luther also had to deal with this accusation in his disputes with the antinomians. There he refuted the related falsehoods that the Law is absolutely necessary to drive our reluctant old nature, and that without that guidance Christian behavior would necessarily disappear.

To add to this already vexed situation (as is always the case), God's ways and human ways are related by contradiction. Thus, the scriptural position is completely nonintuitive! But does scriptural strangeness warrant such considered and comprehensive opposition?

The Relation Between the Holy Spirit and the Law

When it comes to Christian ethics or behavior, a clear contrast is made in Scripture between the agencies of the Holy Spirit and the Law. Everywhere in Scripture, the Law is given to expose sin. It reveals to us why it is that no matter how hard we try, we cannot keep any of our moral resolutions. The Law shows us the way we should live, but it is completely unable to get us there. In that way the Law only makes matters worse. But with the advent of the Holy Spirit on Pentecost (significantly, coming on the very festival of the giving of the Law), God is demonstrating the power of having a new heart. Only because of that new heart is it possible for a new covenant to begin between us. It is a covenant where faith in Jesus's righteousness creates a new heart and new desires. We discover that *we can* rather than *we must*. There is a critical contrast between the Law's impotent *we must* and the newly freed action created by the freedom from the Law through Jesus's imputed righteousness. Only the Holy Spirit creates the faith that *we can* present ourselves to God as those who have been brought from death to life, and that *we can* present our members to God as instruments for righteousness (Rom 6:13). The deliverance from our former slavery to sin, together with the resulting freedom, creates the vital difference in shaping renewed Christian action. Christians trust in the power of the Holy Spirit to lead them. They also trust his working in our hearts, to prevent them from "doing what they would" (Gal 5:17).

Two Metaphors

Two metaphors may be helpful here. The essential difference between a swimmer and a non-swimmer is that a swimmer is completely comfortable with the notion that the water will hold one up. A non-swimmer, on the other hand, is terrified that this is not the case, and thrashes about in the water trying to hold their face out at all costs, using all sorts of self-defeating motions that end up actually opposing the hoped for salvation from the feared drowning. In just the same manner we approach the question of the Law versus the indwelling Holy Spirit's work in a Christian. Which one can produce the desired effect? The Spirit? The Law? A combination of the two? The third choice is, unfortunately and unbiblically, the reigning theological position, which results in much thrashing around to create human righteousness. But that is precisely what the Law exposes as an impossibility. And that is precisely why we need another righteousness—the righteousness of Jesus. Paul makes his most densely stated thesis statement of his preaching in three places. They are all virtually identical. Each of the citations from Rom 3:21, Gal 2:16, and Phil 3:9, preclude any possibility of righteousness flowing from the Law!

Pietists simply cannot believe that the Holy Spirit either knows his job or can accomplish it without our help. So, in their fear and thrashing around, they reintroduce the Law as the salvation from their fear. They hold that unless there is the Law to function as our guide, Christian ethics will have no shape. By insisting that some human lawful cooperation in the new ethics is necessary, they hope to keep from sinking and to keep their faces out of the water. Instead of *You must, You should*, or *You need to*, the gospel encourages us with *You can!* by what is already in you. You can trust the indwelling Holy Spirit to hold you up without your assistance.

A second metaphor can be used to demonstrate how the new Pauline ethic of the Holy Spirit is both organic and miraculous, in the same way that plants growing are organic and miraculous. For instance, a little child might think that pulling on a carrot top might help it to grow, using the childlike logic that since there is a whole world of "magic," maybe we can do something to help that miracle of growth. Adults have learned that there are some things like that which we simply cannot accomplish, even with all our vaunted scientific achievements. The single parable of Mark, which is not copied by Matthew and Luke, makes the same point:

Jesus also said, "This is what the kingdom of God is like. A man scatters seed on the ground. Night and day, whether he sleeps or gets up, the seed sprouts and grows, *though he does not know how. All by itself*, the soil produces grain—first the stalk, then the head, then the full kernel in the head. As soon as the grain is ripe, he puts the sickle to it, because the harvest has come." (Mark 4:26–29; italics added)

In the following chapters I will argue in detail Paul's position on the function of the Law in the life of a Christian, which will be followed by Luther's articulation of the same. Hopefully, the following chapters will demonstrate that Paul's position on the Law has very rarely been clearly and correctly portrayed. What is at issue here is nothing less than proper Christian assurance! When one hears Paul's preaching twisted by human fears or through willful mistranslation, proper Christian assurance is left founded on sandy ground and not upon the one true Rock. When the storms come (most essentially one's last moment) what is going to hold?

Chapter 2

Pietism and the Third Use of the Law

> Christ is the end of the law for all who believe.
>
> Romans 10:4

The Third Use of the Law

For non-theologians a further review is necessary regarding the Lutheran uses of the Law. Lutherans hold that God's word arrives as two contrasting *events*—the word that kills, and the word that gives life. These are respectively termed Law and gospel. The Law is necessary to reveal to us the sin that we hide from, completely deny, or are unable to recognize. This Law word necessarily drives us to Christ, since we are unable to forgive ourselves or to act in proper obedience. The Law indicates our complete inability to be humanly righteous. The Law is vital to prepare us to properly hear the next word of deliverance. The Law drives us to the only conclusion available to sinners, that we will die! Only with this preparation does the second word, the gospel word of deliverance from death, have its heavenly meaning. The forgiveness of Jesus Christ and the gift of his alien righteousness is the only key to life eternal.

The argument in this book is that in Luther's entire theological writings, God's word of Law has only two functions. The first use of the Law is the civil use, to keep society safe (Rom 13:1). For this we have police, judges, prisons, and the armed forces. The ongoing restraint provided by the first use of the Law is necessary because as the historian Will Durant wrote, "Civilization is an occasional and temporary interruption of the jungle."[1]

---

1. Durant, *Our Oriental Heritage*, 226.

The second use of the Law is the theological use, to drive us to Christ. This was described above. What is at issue in this controversy is whether or not there even exists a third use of the Law.

The third-use-of-the-Law position is fully described, defended, and insisted upon, even for Christians, in appendix I at the end of this book. In short, the third use demands the that the Law is required to guide or to drive the ethical life of the renewed Christian. This teaching insists that humanity can only be driven by threat, and that therefore without the Law's guidance, Christian life would devolve into lawlessness and anarchy. People who disagree with this teaching are termed *gospel reductionists*. More commonly they are accused of being antinomian (Greek for "against the Law"[2]). This false accusation is put forward despite that fact that true Reformation Christians, of all creatures on the planet, are most aware of the painful presence and activity of the Law in their lives and conscience. They correctly suffer from it, fulfilling Paul's description of real Christianity, that in our anguish we cry out "Abba Father!" (Rom 8:15–16). Paul asserts here that this cry of experiencing personal failure is the most unassailable warrant that we are actually God's children! Pietists always take the reverse position—they are more interested in the human improvement project, which is decidedly not about failure.

Pietism, together with its theology, is the most quintessential expression of the third use of the Law to be found in all of Christendom. Pietism requires the third use of the Law. The two doctrines of Pietism and the third use of the Law are so inseparably linked as to be synonymous. *Therefore, from now on the two terms will be treated interchangeably.* Many theologians will object that this definition is too simplistic. However, treating the two as almost congruent in their readings of Scripture more clearly reveals the single problem affecting them both.

The presenting problem is that this third use can be found neither in Scripture nor in any of Luther's writings! This teaching found its way into Lutheranism as only as an addendum to the Lutheran Confessions. It was added only after Luther's death. It was never Luther's teaching, nor was it included in the definitive expression of the more Reformation positions—the Augsburg Confession or Luther's Smalcald Articles. I will demonstrate that it could never have existed as Luther's teaching. Nothing like this exists in either Luther's Large or Small Catechisms. Luther's late-in-life definitive teaching on the function of the Law in a Christian's

---

2. BAGD, s.v. "νόμος."

ethical walk is found in the several *Antinomian Disputations*. There he clearly and absolutely excludes such a doctrinal position.

The Gnesio-Lutherans Versus the Philippists

In the two decades after Luther's death in 1546, Melanchthon, Luther's brilliant linguistic professor and architect of the Augsburg Confession, took up the leadership mantle in resolving some still incompletely formed Reformation doctrinal issues. Five controversies needed resolution, including whether Christ was truly present in the Lord's Supper, and whether there was indeed a third use of the Law. Melanchthon took the wrong side on both of these two issues. In the first case, Luther had, like a broken record, in the 1520s debates with Swiss theologian Zwingli, asserted that Jesus said, "This *is* my body." Nowhere does Jesus say, "This *represents* or this *symbolizes* my body." (Once at a Naval facility in San Diego I followed a good Calvinist chaplain down a communion line hearing him say repeatedly, "This represents the body of Christ.") But if this sacramental gift merely represents his body, where is Jesus? Evidently two thousand years ago he was serving this meal. Either that, or he is in heaven, but he is certainly not *here*. Evidently, we are doing this only in *remembrance of him*. The real touchable presence of Christ, *here* and *now* is the issue. It is notable that Melanchthon, the incredibly high IQ professor, always seems to trust reason rather than mystery, and logic over scriptural revelation. His default position for every theological controversy is compromise—something he probably learned from his two mentors, Reuchlin and Erasmus.

In this first doctrinal issue, Melanchthon took his default compromise position, holding that Christ was present only spiritually, which any believer can enjoy, rather than Christ being physically and corporally present in the bread and wine. So, once again in compromise, Melanchthon bravely holds that Christ is "sort of" present! Thus, he denied the more difficult assertion that Christ was physically present in the bread and wine—the position both Luther and the Gnesio-Lutherans (the genuine Lutherans) understand from Scripture.

The "real presence" question at issue is vital! The question at issue is: Is there the no place where a Christian, in this spiritual walk, can find a *touchable* place where he can say with assurance, "I know that this is where the Holy God is *here, for me*"? Two Old Testament narratives demonstrate this continuing human need. Jacob, after experiencing the vision of the ladder to heaven and hearing of God's promise of continued blessing, constructs a mound of stones over that *place*, and pours oil over it, and calls it Bethel—that is, "This is the very house of God" (Gen 28:15–19). Evidently, touchable stones are important, even before Jesus gave his continuing touchability in the physical sacraments of baptism and the Lord's Supper. Again, Naaman, the major general healed by Elisha, asks for two sacks of dirt to be taken home from the front yard (2 Kgs 5:17)! Why? Evidently, he wanted something to touch, tied to the *place* where the Holy God had met him graciously. However, this first doctrinal dispute, regarding the real presence of Christ, is for another place and requires a far more extended discussion.

We move now to the issue at hand, the imagined third use of the Law. In this debate the two parties were, again, the Gnesio-Lutherans against the Philippists. Philip was Melanchthon's first name, thus, the Genuine Lutherans against Melanchthon.

Melanchthon's insistence upon a third use of the Law is fear-based. He cannot conceive of realistic human obedience without the fear and coercion of the Law. The most definitive description of Pietism (ironically, a "Lutheran" doctrinal invention) came about when the Gnesio-Lutherans lost the debate to the Philippists, and Melanchthon's creation of Article VI of the Formula of Concord (appendix I) was enshrined as the official Reformation position. Article VI is Pietism defined.

The fear-based doctrine of Pietism is articulated most clearly in paragraph 1 of Article VI, where it is asserted that it is necessary for Christians "to learn from the Law to live and walk in the Law." But this is moralism, once again. More importantly, his phrase demonstrates the fear that the Holy Spirit neither knows his job, nor is able to create the new joyful obedience in Christians. Obedience and its source and agent are the issue. Is the new obedience created by Christ alone, or is it a cooperative effort on the part of our will?

Again it is asserted that Pietists hold that both the incentive power of the gospel *and* the criterion of the Law are operative in sanctification.

Note the cooperation of agencies required in this definition. God's work alone is the gospel. But here, our work is required to be included in our rescue, through our following the Law's direction. Sometimes Pietists, to avoid using the term *cooperate*, substitute the phrase "we participate." In both cases, the teaching remains that God's agency cooperates with human agency. This is the poison of Pietism. It utterly rejects and refutes Paul's summary statement against his opponents in Gal 2:21: "If righteousness were through the law, Christ died for no purpose."

A fuller description of Pietism includes the following features:

1. **Emphasis on Personal Conversion**
   - Pietism teaches that personal conversion, a heartfelt experience of salvation, is essential. This conversion involves our intellectual assent to doctrines, but also should include an inward, transformative experience of God's grace. Individuals must feel and experience the reality of God's love in their hearts. (As always, "they must!")

2. **The Centrality of Scripture**
   - Pietists believe that the Bible is the ultimate authority for Christian life and practice. Personal Bible reading and meditation on Scripture are encouraged to foster a deeper connection with God. It's not merely about intellectual knowledge but about spiritual transformation through Scripture.

3. **Living Out a Holy Life**
   - True faith, according to Pietism, leads to a transformed life. Pietists believe that salvation is not merely about believing the right doctrines but about living according to God's will. This means striving for holiness, moral purity, and ethical behavior in everyday life. The Christian life is to be marked by active love, humility, and service to others.

4. **The Priesthood of All Believers**
   - Pietism affirms the idea that all Christians are called to live out their faith and minister to others, not just the clergy. Every believer has direct access to God and is responsible for their spiritual growth and for the encouragement of others in the faith. This is connected to the idea of small fellowship groups where Christians meet regularly for prayer, Bible study, and mutual support.

5. **Emotional and Experiential Faith**
   - While not dismissing doctrinal understanding, Pietism emphasizes the importance of emotional and experiential aspects of faith. Pietists seek not only a rational understanding of God but

a deep, heartfelt experience of God's presence and transforming power. This emphasis on inner spiritual life distinguishes them from the more formal, intellectual approaches to religion.

6. **Spiritual Renewal and Revival**
   - Pietism is, at its heart, a movement of spiritual renewal within the church. It calls for a return to the authentic Christian life as modeled in the New Testament, where true Christianity is seen in transformed lives, rather than in mere ritual or empty tradition. This desire for renewal sometimes led to revivalist movements, such as the Great Awakening of the eighteenth century together with most revival movements and their camp meetings in the United States in the following centuries.

7. **The Role of Grace**
   - Like other forms of Protestantism, Pietism holds that salvation is a gift of God's grace, not based on human merit or works. However, Pietists stresses that God's grace, while freely given, *must* lead to an active response of faith and moral transformation. Salvation is both a gift and a call to live out God's will.

8. **Focus on the Holy Spirit**
   - Pietism places strong emphasis on the role of the Holy Spirit in the life of the believer. The Spirit is seen as the agent of transformation, guiding Christians toward a deeper relationship with God and empowering them to live holy lives. Spiritual gifts, including a deep sense of personal conviction and a life of prayer, are understood as signs of the Holy Spirit's work in the believer.

9. **Mission and Evangelism**
   - Pietism encourages Christians to share their faith actively, not just through words but through a life that reflects the love and power of Christ. Evangelism is not only about preaching but also about living as a witness to the truth of the gospel in every sphere of life. This often includes involvement in social issues and caring for the marginalized.

In summary, the theology of Pietism can be understood as a holistic approach to the Christian life, one that involves personal conversion, deep devotional life, ethical living, and spiritual transformation through the power of the Holy Spirit. While it remains a critique of intellectualism and formalism, Pietism does not reject doctrine or the church. Instead, it seeks to reinvigorate them through an emphasis on personal faith and spiritual experience.

What is completely ironic here is the Pietist's salutary emphasis upon the Holy Spirit. Pietists insist upon his presence and work continually, while at the same time refusing to believe that the Holy Spirit knows his job! And the Spirit's job is fulsomely described in Gal 5, where Paul lays out the sevenfold fruit of the Spirit—undreamed of, unheard of, and unachievable under the Law. If the Holy Spirit can miraculously and organically produce all that, why then is the Law still a continued necessary agent or guide in producing all these "Christian Athlete" efforts? Why is the Law still necessary to produce some new human righteousness progress demanded by the Pietist?

Evidence that the preacher is a Pietist always comes out in proclamation. I listened to a twenty-two-minute sermon by a fellow Lutheran that had thirty-two instances of these terms in that time frame:

- It is mandatory (one time)
- There ought to be (three times)
- There is to be (two times)
- We ought (three times)
- We should (two times)
- Try to (two times)
- What if? (one time)
- We need to (two times)
- We would be if (five times)
- There must be (one time)
- We have to (one time)
- We must (two times)
- Do we? (four times)
- We are to be (two times)
- What have you done? (one time)

These are all words of Law requiring performance, which, under the Law, have to be exactly fulfilled or else! Surely the example above demonstrates that this controversy is no arcane or ancillary theological problem! Such preaching has inevitable and destructive effects for the Christian hearer, who thinks that they are hearing the gospel! In an Alabama location where I preached for seven years, the Sunday noon tradition was for families to gather to eat out at restaurants after church. However, these restaurant servers expressed to me their holy terror over their Sunday morning duties. Why? Because their clientele, on Sunday noon, too often came in spitting mad. But what caused this? Certainly what they heard at church, under the guise of gospel grace, was having the very opposite effect of joy. The Law *always* has the same negative effect. It is our sworn enemy. As Luther said, "Lex semper accusat," the Law always accuses. And that makes all who are accused very angry and defensive. They always seek some way to escape its damning verdict. But there is no escape. The impossibility of escape is built into God's basic design of the Law. To refuse to recognize that simple fact makes one a Pietist.

The Two Opposing Ditches Misrepresenting Paul's Teaching of the Law: Pietism and Antinomianism.

You will note, especially in numbers 1, 3, 5, and 6 in the list above, the Pietist's deep conviction that the church needs to reform from mere formalism (ridiculed as "chancel prancing") and evidence-free claims of faith. These, and other similar dangers, they cynically consign to the catchall sin of formalism or antinomianism. Pietism seeks to rescue us from that. That is their first fear. But is it accurate to present, as the only other alternative, the opposite ditch of antinomianism? (The ditch of antinomianism will be explored in chapter 8 detailing Luther's response in his *Antinomian Disputations*.)

Another Pietist fear is that we need rescuing from the theology of God's election. They hold that God's election just will not work unless we accept it. Our salvific rescue must have a human agency in cooperation with God's work. If not in the justifying part (Lutheran Pietists), then at least in the sanctifying part! See numbers 1, 3, 7, and 8 above.

Pelagianism, Pietism, moralism, and Lutheran orthodoxy all have the same mother, and sing the same tune, which they play over and over again:

1) God's grace is presented as an *offer* rather than a mercifully completed and done deed via election. But, an offer is not yet the gift! An offer requires the validating human response—the cooperation!

2) In our sanctification—that is, our new ethical Christian behavior—we are required to trust the Law's guidance to produce what it never can produce, and never has produced. Worse, Pietism distrusts the Spirit to produce the fruit of the Spirit organically, without our help.

3) Human righteousness and Jesus's righteousness are combined rather than understood as annihilating each other because they are two completely different entities.

4) The Law is presented as our friend rather than being our mortal enemy, whose God-given function is only to make matters worse, so that we would be driven to another righteousness.

5) And election is insisted upon as our choice, rather than God's. "Accepting Jesus as our personal Savior" (American syncretism) is presented as the first critical step in our salvation. Instead of our cooperation, what God has provided to save us is the *absolution*, purely and simply declared. Instead of the sinner's prayer, the absolution can be spoken in some such fashion as this:

    "I announce and declare to you: 'Jesus loves sinners! You qualify! After all, sinners are the only people God can find! God has forgiven your sins, because Jesus has died on the cross for you! Your sins were taken away there. God has chosen you! I have been sent to give you this personal, assured word from God to you. You can trust God's word, because God does not lie!'"

Anything that follows that statement is purely God's work. Our insistence upon some human requirement to validate such an absolution will come back to haunt that person with the inevitable question, "Was my 'acceptance' of Jesus warm-hearted enough?" That is why salvation, together with its required election, must be by God alone. Sola. And, if this whole life of ours is training for our last few seconds on earth, what will your last foundation be for your assurance in that crisis? Each of us faces that crisis alone. "Prepare to meet your God!" cries out the prophet Amos (4:12). Will your warm-hearted "cooperation," even the personal goodness "enabled by the Holy Spirit," stand the test in that moment?

Chapter 3

Melanchthon's Third Use of the Law

To refute and demolish Melanchthon's entire proposition that there is a third use of the Law one must first begin with a clear concept of biblical righteousness and its relation to the Law.

- The righteousness that saves Christians belongs to Jesus alone.
- It does not indwell Christians but rather is imputed, or counted to us.
- This saving righteousness is complete and completed. ("It is finished!" is the Gospel of John's recorded word of Jesus from the cross; 19:30.)
- This righteousness is alien to us, is completely outside of us, and resides in heaven.
- This righteousness is God's 100 percent assault upon our indwelling sin, in that, just as is it impossible to be 85 percent pregnant, it is likewise impossible to be only partially righteous.
- This righteousness cannot be apprehended by any of the five human senses, but it is rather apprehended and made our own by faith alone.
- Such faith is only be made possible by the indwelling of the Holy Spirit and thus becomes the primary evidence that we belong to Christ (Rom 8:9–11).
- This righteousness is by hope, since righteousness becoming our own actual reality lies in the future: "We wait for the hope of righteousness" (Gal 5:5).
- Jesus's righteousness and human righteousness are two separate categories and can never be combined, but rather annihilate each other. "Not having a righteousness of my own, based on law, but that which is through the faith of Jesus" (Phil 3:9; see also vv. 2–8; Rom 3:21–22; Gal 2:16–17; and 3:10–12).

- Nonintuitively, our righteousness is not accomplished by our deeds but, rather, solely by Jesus's deeds! So, *Jesus's* earthly ministry, death, resurrection, ascension to heaven, and sitting at the right hand of God the Father constitute our righteousness (John 16:10).

- Jesus's righteousness separates two periods of history. The coming and advent of this righteousness divides all history into whatever precedes the cross and resurrection of Jesus, and whatever follows. Pentecost, which reveals this with the descent of the Holy Spirit, separates the old covenant from the new covenant, and the Old Testament from the New Testament.

- The Holy Spirit is not, himself, this righteousness, but his coming at Pentecost is necessary because he is the only one who can critically testify to us that we have the righteousness of Jesus.

- Finally, in the matter of ethics, this righteousness renders the function of the Law *obsolete*, since the Law is always limited to being merely ostensive. That is, the Law can only point to, rather than actually produce, righteousness. The Law points a Christian to something that now is fulfilled completely outside of them, in Jesus Christ. When this work of Jesus is apprehended by faith, the Law's function is fulfilled and it has no more to say. *The Law then ceases completely.* The Holy Spirit reveals this new righteousness so surely to each Christian that they somehow surely "know" that this is true. So true that Christians are willing to die for this amazing gift.

This long summary of what is entailed in the sola "righteousness by Christ alone" is the scriptural basis for all Christian assurance, which was championed at great cost by Martin Luther and Reformation pastors, some of whom were burned at the stake for such affirmation.

This entire introduction is meant to serve as a vital contrast, at each point, to the work of Melanchthon, the theological adversary of every syllable of this book. A brief biographical summary of this amazing person is required to give helpful context to the continuing controversy.

Melanchthon's Life Story

Melanchthon was born in 1497, ten years after Martin Luther. He was a certified prodigy, with an IQ probably in the 160s or even the 170s. He entered the university of Heidelberg at age eleven, and got his BA at age twelve. He achieved his MA at Tubingen at age fifteen. While there, his study of theology was led by two mentors—his uncle Reuchlin and the famous humanist and Reformer Erasmus. While there he became convinced that true Christianity differed from the current scholastic doctrines of Thomas Aquinas. Significantly for his later life, he published a book of Greek grammar in 1518. By age twenty-one he, himself, was recognized as a Reformer and accepted a call to be a professor of Greek at the fledgling university at Wittenberg. While there, he became fast friends with Luther, so much so that when Luther was imprisoned at the Wartburg castle for his own safety, Luther turned to Melanchthon to be the leader at the Wittenberg university. But Melanchthon's weak leadership failed the university when the Zwickau Prophets showed up, throwing the whole place into theological confusion. The chaotic result forced Luther to return from exile. By Luther's simple tactic of preaching, he restored the university and the whole town to order, saving it from its wild anarchy.

A pattern began to emerge here that was to describe Melanchthon's character for the rest of his career. As is often the case in every person, their salient strength is at the same time their greatest weakness. In Melanchthon's case, my view is that his immense mental capability led him, at crucial moments in the upcoming Reformation crises, to trust his head far more than his heart. As Luther would put it, he trusted in reason far more than he was willing to trust faith.

One of the ways in which Melanchthon displayed his head-over-heart tendency was his magnum opus from 1521, *Loci communes rerum theologicarum seu hyotyposes theologicae*, a systemization of theology. This work presents a critical difference between Luther and him. Luther was never interested in the systemization of theology, because Luther understood theology more as an encounter with the living Word. This primary understanding of the Word as personal encounter is evident also in the apostle Paul who always addressed each particular situation with the living Word. Paul's only writing that could be construed as systematic theology is the book of Romans, whose purpose was to demonstrate what Paul was preaching everywhere. The danger of systemization is that it tends to render the truth of the gospel into propositional statements that can be stapled and filed and canned for future use. Witness only how Lutheran orthodoxy became so dead in the pursuit of this kind of theology. But this is the propositional head-over-heart kind of stuff that Melanchthon excelled in.

Another of the ways where Melanchthon's trust in his head betrayed him was his everlasting attempt to try to find middle ground in every conflict. Perhaps he learned this from one of his early mentors, Erasmus, whom Luther pilloried as a slippery eel in his treatise *The Bondage of the Will* for his attempts to be acceptable to both sides in the Reformation debate. I cite only three instances of Melanchthon's behavior. The first instance was at the critical Augsburg gathering (1530) that included the attendance of the new Holy Roman Emperor together with virtually the entire leadership of the church at Rome. This gathering was the last hope for retaining the unity of the church, to keep it from splitting into two opposing theologies. Luther, who was kept at a safe distance away from this gathering by reason of the threat to his life by the government ban, was in anguish that Melanchthon would give away too much important theological ground to the Roman theologians in his characteristic attempts to find the middle ground. Although Luther's work formed the basis for the presented Augsburg Confession, Melanchthon was its final author. Luther did not conceal his dissatisfaction with its irenic tone. The Reformation position was maintained, however, resulting in the split of the two theological positions.

Fast forward thirty-seven years where, nineteen years after Luther's death, Melanchthon was still the default leader. In my view, the character of his leadership once again shipwrecked the Reformation. Among the controversies in the competing positions of the incompletely formed Reformation theology were the questions of the real presence of Christ in the Lord's Supper and Melanchthon's opinion that good works are necessary for salvation. In the first controversy, the Gnesio-Lutherans (the genuine Lutherans) versus the Philippists, Melanchthon predictably chose a middle position in the dispute. As expected, he held that Christ was sort of present in the Lord's Supper—that is, only spiritually. In the second dispute, his middle-of-the-road theological position over whether good works are necessary for salvation produced the third use of the Law—the concern of this entire book. In this case he was accurately accused of synergism (human cooperation in the matters of salvation). In both cases, Melanchthon critically undermined positions vital to Reformation theology taught by his mentor, Martin Luther. These controversies properly embittered him for the rest of his life.

However, his betrayal of the Reformation was not yet complete. He later shamefully compromised other Reformation positions several times in order to avoid controversy when, after Luther's death, horrible persecutions arose against other Lutheran Reformers.

The Counter-Reformation

Here are some key points developed in the resulting Catholic opposition, which, unlike Melanchthon, were made in uncompromising form by church council proceedings. They entail the entire content and substance of the Reformation debate with the church at Rome. Convened after Luther's death, the Council of Trent's twenty-five sessions from 1545 until 1563 had as their sole purpose to refute the central positions of the Reformation teaching.

Session six, January 1547, rightly recognizes that Reformation teaching asserted strenuously that proper Christian assurance was by Christ alone, and that this teaching formed the critical and nonnegotiable assertion of all Reformation teaching. That the Catholics clearly recognize this is evident in the following canons on justification. In contrast to Melanchthon's signature productions, there is no middle road in these declarations:

Canon V: "If any one saith that since Adam's sin, the *free will of man is lost* and extinguished; or, that it is a thing with only a name, yea a name without a reality, a figment, in fine, introduced in the church by Satan; *let him be anathema.*" (Yet this is the central assertion in Luther's magnum opus *The Bondage of the Will* where he asserts that our will does not ever cooperate with God, but, in captivation, always resists God.)

Canon IX: "If any one saith, that *by faith alone the impious is justified*; in such wise as to mean, that nothing else is required to co-operate in order to the obtaining the grace of justification and that it is not in any way necessary, that he be prepared and disposed by the movement of his own will; *let him be anathema.*"

Canon XI: "If any one saith, that *men are justified, either by the sole imputation of the justice of Christ, or by the sole remission of sins*, to the exclusion of the grace and the charity which is poured forth in their hearts by the Holy Ghost, and is inherent in them; or even that the grace, whereby we are justified, is only the favour of God; *let him be anathema.*" (That is, after the fall, humanity retained a divine spark whose will is still able to respond to grace. Therefore, human cooperation of the will is necessary. All the *solas* are thus heretical.)

Canon XVIII: "If anyone saith, that the commandments of God are, even for one that is justified and constituted in grace, impossible to keep; *let him be anathema*."[1]

The issue here is whether the Law continues to function at all in the matter of salvation, and, therefore, whether there is any cooperation by humans in the matter. Luther discovered, through his painful attempts at attaining human righteousness, that believing at all in the smallest cooperation completely jettisons any hope of Christian assurance. Human perfection, here on earth, is just not possible.

So, the central Reformation battle continues. How does one achieve proper Christian assurance? Since the Roman Catholic Church maintains the church councils are inerrant, they are stuck with the Council of Trent, whose canons remove all hope of Christian assurance. If the canons above articulate what constitutes undebatable matters of faith, they show why subsequent efforts to reunite Catholics with Protestants, who hold Luther's actual Reformation position, have inevitably failed.

Canon XVIII introduces the issue of sanctification. Philip Melanchthon, in typical fashion, sort of agrees with the Catholic position, but not quite. Instead, he reintroduces human cooperation by asserting the necessity of the Law's guidance, but this time only at the level of sanctification rather than at the level of justification. In this benighted effort at moderation in all things, he once again jettisons Christian assurance. That is, he betrays the entire Reformation effort.

It is telling that, in the later controversies, he waits to do this only after Luther's death. Sanctification is all about the new Christian behavior, and thus about ethics. For Melanchthon, if it is about ethics, surely it must mean that the Law is needed!

So, here is the continuing critical post-Reformation question: Is it really true that the good news consists in fact that the Law has now been rendered benign, and is no longer accusatory, but is now rendered helpfully directive for Christians, who know that their righteousness resides in Jesus?

---

1. Wikisource, "Canons"; italics added.

CHAPTER 4

Objections by Pietists to Defend Their Claim That the Law Is Needed to Provide Structure and Guidance for Christian Ethics

There Are Over One Hundred Commands in Paul's Letters

C. S. LEWIS DESCRIBED JOY as the secret signature of God's presence in the believer's life. Joy is a yearning that points to something eternal. He discovered this joy at one of the darkest points in his life. Nor was it a fleeting happiness, but rather a profound sense of God's nearness, a foretaste of what we are traveling toward. In his book *Surprised by Joy*, the title itself expresses the theme of the entire book, that joy cannot be attained by human effort, but rather comes unexpectedly and graciously. More—it is the beginning fulfillment of all human longing, which no counterfeit can achieve.

The Pietists claim that there are over one hundred commands in Paul's writings. They assert from this that the Law is everywhere present and serves the valid function of guiding the new life of a Christian. To test that assertion, let us look at just one of these "commands." Paul writes as a command, "Rejoice always, and again I say rejoice!" (Phil 4:4).

Certainly, this is a command. But is it a command in any way related to the Law? As noted above, joy is not able to be commanded, but always surprises us and appears only upon God's presence and direction. How odd, then, that it is commanded here! Joy is nowhere even dreamed of in the Ten Commandments, nor is it anywhere in the Torah's directions. When Paul says that we "walk by the Spirit and not by the law" (Gal 5:16–18), note that the only person able to fulfill the command, rejoice, within the Christian is the Holy Spirit and not the Law. The source of this joy is the Holy Spirit's own presence and work, and has absolutely no relation to the Law. The "command" here is to discover and exercise what you already have!

Many more examples, similar to this, can be adduced. Conclusion: these "over one hundred commands" found in the apostle Paul's letters arise from a source other than the Law, and thus cannot be argued as evidence of the continuing necessity and presence of the Law, understood as a commandment, in the walk of a Christian. This joy resides in the gospel-country of *because-therefore*, and not in the Law-country of *if-then*. This joy resides in the country of *You can*, rather than in the country of *You must, you need to, or you should*. The *xoris* (Greek for apart from the Law)[1] of Rom 3:28 is being practically demonstrated here and everywhere in the rest of these "commands." Christian ethics are not only possible apart from the Law, but necessarily have to be completely separated from the Law, in order to create the freedom of the new Christian walk (Gal 5:1).

We come now to the fact that Paul has a concept called the Law of Christ (Gal 6:2; Rom 13:8–10). In Rom 5:20–21 and in 1 Cor 15:56, Paul has identified the two opposing triumvirate kingdoms that define all human reality: *Law-sin-death* versus *grace-righteousness-life*. Each stands unalterably in a war with the other in the human heart and mind. No component part of Law-sin-death can be permitted to transgress into the domain of grace-righteousness-life, or all Christian freedom is lost. That is the critical argument of Rom 6, 7, and 8.

So, if the Law is not allowed into the grace-righteousness-life ethics of a Christian, how can there be a Law of Christ? This Law of Christ must be a new power of some kind. And it is. No legalistic observance is being described by this term, but rather a shorthand description of the Holy Spirit himself, describing the Spirit's power to create in us the fruit listed in Gal 5—love, joy, peace, patience, kindness, goodness, faithfulness, gentleness, and self-control. This fruit fulfills the true intent of the Law. The Law could never have produced a single one of these characteristics in a human being. "So faith, hope, and love abide, but the greatest of these is love" (1 Cor 13:13) is another expression of the Law of Christ inhabiting the human heart.

---

1. BAGD, s.v. "χωρίς."

Human obedience is the critical issue in contention here. The Pietist is unalterably convinced that obedience does not and cannot exist without the threat of the Law. Paul's contrasting argument is that the Holy Spirit creates a new heart that has new desires and new motivations. A Christian loves the Lord Jesus and wants to follow him. This new longing and desire are critical. They could never be created by threat or terror or accusation. This following together with the whole of the new obedience is characterized by this desire. When Jesus says, "Take up your cross and follow me" (Matt 16:24; Luke 9:23), it is not, as the Pietist understands this, as "Just in case there is any persecution," (as if the Law is his friend and the cross is not the current pain). However, what happens daily to a Christian who is paying any attention is that his faith is *suffering*. Why? Because the Law is doing its correct function, by killing the old self so that the new can arise. The suffering that this daily execution causes is unavoidable. That is why a Christian cries, "Abba, Father!" (Rom 8:15–16).

There was much disobedience in Paul's churches after he left them. In Corinth alone there were antinomians who declared that the freedom of the gospel, with its absence of all Law, allowed sensual behaviors of all kinds. There were divisive, competing claims falsely rooting authority in the persons who had baptized them. There was insistence that quarrels among the saints be adjudicated by authorities of the Law. There was the everlasting Jewish claim that circumcision was vital and necessary to the saving covenant. There was the question of whether eating foods that had been offered to idols was sanctioned in a Christian's freedom. There was idolatry and misuse of the Lord's Supper. Yet, never once in all of these questions, which evidently cry out for empirical solution by some command or Law, did Paul ever use or adduce the Law as a solution to any of these problems.

Paul's solution was always that since we have died with Christ and that we have been baptized into Christ, we are now obedient to Christ with a new obedience of living under the Holy Spirit. He uses his apostolic authority to deliver the word of Jesus's promise into each situation. Sometimes he admits that he doesn't have that clear word, but he gives direction by his own insight.

The impressive revelation to us is that in each letter of Paul there is obedience without the Law. This obedience takes its characteristic shape from the fact that it is not driven by threat, but by a new desire to follow Jesus on the same path that he took—through death to life. Christians are not lawless.

But Jesus Says, "Observe All I Have Commanded You."

Pietists use Matt 28:20, where Jesus, in his farewell address, says, "Teaching them to observe all that I have commanded you," to make the case that Christians are newly able to be Law followers.

This verse is cited by Pietists as definitive proof that the Law has a vital role in guiding Christian behavior. However, if one checks out the preceding Sermon on the Mount, Matthew's set piece in chapter 5 to interpret the Ten Commandments, such a claim is simply not possible.

The case cannot be made from Matthew's Gospel that "all that I have commanded you" refers to the Torah or the Ten Commandments. In the Sermon on the Mount, we hear Jesus tightening up the Law, in order to demonstrate that the Law is no one's friend, not even for a Christian. Rather the Law is everywhere our *executioner*, and nothing less. Every time Jesus says, "But I say to you," it is a breathtaking accusation—an authoritative claim only possible if it is made by the One who gave the Law in the first place. And every time Jesus says, "But I say to you," every one of the Ten Commandments becomes even more impossible for any human to fulfill. Even former president Jimmy Carter, a pious Baptist, confessed that Jesus's interpretation of the commandment regarding adultery hopelessly convicted him. If "everyone who looks at a woman lustfully has already committed adultery with her in his heart" (Matt 5:28), he expressed his personal anxiety before those incriminating words. Implicitly, he thus acknowledged the impossibility of fulfilling this Law as stated and interpreted by Jesus.

Jesus continues interpreting the Law in its rightful God-given and heavenly function—to execute us. With hammer blow after hammer blow, Jesus does the same thing with every one of his six "But I say to you's" in Matt 5:17–48. Each of the Ten Commandments under Jesus's review and heavenly interpretation becomes humanly unachievable. *That is the whole point.* They are meant to be diagnostic only ("You are sick!") and not directive. The verses that bookend this section of the Sermon underline that essential truth. First, Jesus says,

> Therefore whoever relaxes one of the least of these commandments and teaches others to do the same will be called the least in the kingdom of heaven, but whoever does them and teaches them will be called great in the kingdom of heaven. For I tell you, unless your righteousness exceeds that of the scribes and

Pharisees, you will never[, ever] enter the kingdom of heaven. (vv. 19-20; my translation of the emphatic Greek *ou me*)

And second, Jesus affirms, "You, therefore, must be perfect as your heavenly Father is perfect" (Matt 5:48).

But that perfection is exactly what is being hopelessly evaded by Pietists in their delusion that behaving better now will suffice. There is a cost for this. In insisting upon some kind of lawful improvement project, they join Jimmy Carter in his anxiety. Worse, as the thesis of this entire book seeks to demonstrate, they lose all hope of proper Christian certainty and assurance.

Those bookend verses require something far beyond human righteousness. They point to the hope of another righteousness, one that does not belong to us, one that is counted to us. That is also the point, always evaded by Pietists who insist upon a theology of a remaining possibility of human perfectability or human righteousness. John Wesley's hope was that with the indwelling Spirit's help we could be launched on a human-righteousness project by using Methodism. But this theology cannot be made to comport or agree with Jesus's clear word that "you must be perfect as your heavenly Father is perfect." Clearly such perfection is humanly unachievable, even with the most piously lived life under the Holy Spirit's direction!

Therefore, Matthew's concluding proclamation is the same as Paul's. There are only two righteousnesses. One righteousness is *human*, while the other belongs to *Jesus alone*. The two can never be combined. One will always annihilate the other. Seeking to amalgamate or combine the two runs into Paul's shocking condemnation, "If righteousness were through the law, then Christ died for no purpose" (Gal 2:28), leaving one single urgent question: "Which righteousness do you believe?"

The Vital Distinction Between Law and Gospel

Lutherans are taught in preaching to carefully distinguish between Law and gospel. Although that precise distinction resides finally and essentially in the work of the Holy Spirit, we are given some pretty good markers to assist the process during proclamation. One marker is for the preacher (you, whenever you bear witness) to note first the *effect* that each word of God has on you. For the word is written to you. It is a letter where God communicates to you personally, and it is not merely a "text."

So, what does this word of God *do* to you? Does it kill (Law)? Does it make alive (gospel)? Those are two of the salient markers to help make that critical distinction, before one comes to proclamation or witnessing.

After arriving at that distinction, another axiom is put in place—that the gospel always is the last word. The gospel follows the Law. But without the Law's killing, with its necessary and inevitable execution of our false hopes, lies, and delusions, there is no good news. God's fearful, accusatory Law is always preparatory to the continuing and desperate prayer of a Christian: "Create in me a clean heart, O God, and renew a right spirit within me" (Ps 51:10). The Law must never follow the absolution nor become the warrant for the absolution. The axiom that the gospel is always the last word is foundational to any possible Christian assurance. This is especially true in the last moments of your life.

So, why does the first of Matthew's five sermons by Jesus end with such a mighty crash? "And great was the fall of it!" (Matt 7:27). This sounds a lot like the last word is the Law! But that is only apparent. The crash of the house built upon sand only more urgently highlights that there is a foundational Rock for you. His name is Jesus. Believe him! Live, each day, believing and resting upon the rock of his righteousness alone! The gospel always has the merciful last word.

We return again to Jesus's last word, in Matthew: "Teaching them to observe all that I have commanded you" (Matt 28:20). This simply cannot be interpreted to mean that we are now empowered to observe the Ten Commandments with a new and improved human righteousness. As evidenced, at the very least, in his first sermon, "All I have commanded you" begins and ends by directing our faith to Jesus and his work, rather than upon our human work. Christians are founded upon the rock of Jesus's righteousness, and not upon the Law's human righteousness.

The Pietist's Favorite Book—James

The book of James begins by affirming, with Paul, the primacy and centrality of faith (1:3, 6) and the centrality of the cross with its attendant suffering (1:9–12). Pietists, by their misreading and false interpretation, falsely make the book of James into their ally. They hear James defending the position that the Law is a Christian's friend rather than that the Law, in its heaven-sent function, is the executioner of the entire human race's pretensions of righteousness. But this majority misreading is based solely upon an untenable presupposition, that James's unique phrases—"mirror" (1:23) and "the law of liberty" (1:25)—both refer to the Torah. If so, then James simply cannot be made to be congruent, consistent, coherent, or consonant with Paul's theology. In fact, the two preachers become diametrically opposed to each other. Such a fundamental disagreement not only undermines scriptural integrity but, worse, also damns any hope of assurance based upon scriptural reliability. That such a misreading is so easy to do is what caused Luther to characterize James as "a right strawy epistle."[2]

Clearly, James asserts that some renewed ethical activity is vitally important, to show that faith is not an evidence-free claim. James writes, "But be doers of the word and not hearers only, deceiving yourselves" and "Faith apart from works is dead" (1:22 and again in 2:14–26). Does not the apostle Paul everywhere warn of the very same thing? But Pietists read James as a necessary corrective to Paul's theology, which they fear can be dangerously misread to produce antinomian behavior. Critical to understand here is that every Pietist argument is always fear-based!

"It is not power that corrupts, but fear. Fear of losing power corrupts those who wield it. Fear of the scourge of power corrupts those who are subject to it," says the very persecuted Aung San Suu Kyi.[3] Taking her observation into theology is instructive. Here, humans are corrupted by their fear of ceding their power to God, regarding the choice of their salvation. In fearful defense mechanism, some find comfort by their election of God, insisting upon human power over our salvific destiny, rather than trusting in God's faithfulness. Lutherans call this decision theology.

Basic logic demonstrates that if one starts with the wrong presupposition, one will inevitably end up with the wrong conclusion. James clearly says, "Be doers of the *word*." Pietists jump to the interpretation that this "word" means the "Law" rather than the gospel word of freedom, which is described by Paul in the whole book of Galatians. Only then can they go on to claim that it is the *Law* that is the agent or director of such Christian activity. They claim further that this is proof that

- the Law is a necessary guide for the renewed Christian's life, and
- that there is, therefore, such a thing a human righteousness.

---

2. *LW* 35:362.
3. Aung San Suu Kyi, *Freedom*, 180.

Only if one begins with the presuppositions that each of James's phrases refers to the Torah can James's critical phrases, the "mirror" (1:23) and the "perfect law, the law of liberty" (1:25), support this third use of the Law as a guide for Christian ethics.

Because Pietists assume that the mirror is synonymous with Law, then it can be understood as the how-to guide for Christians. However, James asserts that the function of this mirror is something that you look into *to show you who you are.* (1:24) Clearly, the word of God arrives as an event that both kills and makes alive—that is, it arrives as both Law and gospel. The mirror, in James, cannot be limited to just one of these functions. So, yes, looking into the word as a mirror shows clearly that you are a sinner. However, that is only the *first* of its necessary functions, and only *half* of its revelation of who you are. Should that be all that this mirror word reveals of who you are then it would be a lie. The complete, accompanying gospel word also reveals to you that, through Jesus's righteousness, you are at the same time a sinner *and* a justified person. Only when *both sides* of your redeemed person are revealed is the mirror word revealing the truth. This complete revelation of the mirror prevents one from being the "hearer who forgets" and rather creates a "doer who acts" (1:25).

Next, the Law of liberty, central to the preceding argument, is once again similarly misinterpreted and defined by Pietists as synonymous with the Commandments. The fact that this simply makes no possible logical sense is no hindrance to them! Explain, then, how the Law can be the Law of "liberty"! *Law of liberty* is an oxymoron, if understood as referring to the Commandment. Where there is Law there is no liberty. Just as light and darkness or up and down are complete opposites, so are Law and liberty (Gal 5:1). Paul rightly notes that the Law was given only to make matters worse, and to expose what every sinner denies and would rather cover up. "The power of sin is the law" (1 Cor 15:56)! The Law can only expose that we are helpless slaves! It is restricted by God to being diagnostic, and not directive! Terms such as *a liberating Law* or *a Law of liberty* have to be oxymorons, and are thus utterly impossible, if interpreted as synonymous with Torah. *The Law liberates no one.* Only Jesus can do that. Therefore, the Law of liberty has to be James's nomenclature to describe that something new and different has arrived. Rather, it has to be his term to describe the new principle of our gospel deliverance.

We now arrive at the most dangerous sentence in James. "You see that a person is justified by works and not by faith alone" (2:24). Pietists read the first part of this sentence as if it stands alone. It does not. This sentence merely summarizes the preceding argument that Abraham and Rahab demonstrated their faith by their works. More, when James writes of Abraham that "faith was active along with his works and faith was completed by his works; and the Scripture was fulfilled that says, 'Abraham believed God, and it was counted to him as righteousness'" (2:22–23), James acknowledges that faith (three times!) is primary and shows itself in the works it produces.

Paul would be unhappy with the summary phrasing of verse 24, to be sure. But, in James, faith remains still as the sole producer of the product. Faith is the agent, and not works. More critically, what James here refers to as works is what Paul calls the organically produced fruit of the Spirit—love, joy, peace, patience, kindness, goodness, faithfulness, gentleness, and self-control. Where these are evident, you know that you are a child of God, because only the Spirit can produce these things (Rom 8:9). The emphatic, and correct, argument that James is seeking to make is that the two—faith and the accompanying fruit of the Spirit—are inseparable. Faith justifies. But real faith is always accompanied by what it alone produces.

What is at issue in James's whole argument is that some people have been making evidence-free claims to him that they have faith. The problem here is that the presence of faith or its absence cannot be determined by any empirical evidence, since faith is invisible to any of our human senses. Therefore, the only evidence that qualifies is what genuine faith always produces—works. For example, no Israelite spy could look into Rahab's heart. James's argument is that her actions alone empirically revealed her faith. His solidly scriptural assertion is that the two—faith and its resulting works—are inseparable. Since they are inseparable, it results in his statement above, "You see, that a person is justified by works and not by faith alone" (v. 24). Then follows the statement, "In the same way was not also Rahab the prostitute justified by works when she received the messengers and sent the out by another way?" (v. 25). Notice here that James contributes the fact that she was and remains a prostitute in doing this. That detail proves that this cannot be the argument that her personal righteousness saved her!

So this is a long, long way from reading James's argument as saying (without the critical qualification of faith) that

- "Works justify"; or
- that, implicitly, "Works are equivalent to the faith that produces them"; or
- that "Works *cooperate* with faith to make faith salvific" (scholastic doctrine).

These are among claims that are triumphantly and falsely insisted upon by Pietists.

The phrase "But be doers of the word and not hearers only, deceiving yourselves" acknowledges that the actions arising from the Holy Spirit's work comes from *hearing*. But the first word that faith hears is that *Jesus* is our righteousness! This righteousness does not consist of human actions, nor is this righteousness anywhere described as a cooperation with rectified human activity (central to Pietist theology). Scripture is everywhere clear that Jesus's righteousness and human righteousness are two antithetical entities. Hearing via the Holy Spirit produces the human actions that only arise from the faith that our righteousness resides in another. Because our righteousness is already complete, these actions take on a completely different motive and heart, unrecognized and unavailable to any conception of the Pietist. These "Holy Spirit actions" are newly done in complete and joyful freedom. This freedom, as contrasted to acts done under the threatening of the Law, is what makes the new "doing" different in kind from the old Law-based human ethics.

If this is the case, then being *doers* of the word (of faith) is done by "walking by the Spirit" (to use Paul's vocabulary in Gal 5:16). This doing is not by the Law, but consists of everything done that arises from the faith that you have Jesus's righteousness. It all depends upon how one interprets James's definition of being doers of the *word*. Which word? Shall we believe he means the word of Law or the word of faith? His unique phrase "the Law of liberty" (used only here in the entire scriptural revelation) cannot be logically made to mean "Law" in the old sense of the Ten Commandments. It has to refer, instead, to the newness that only Jesus introduces. Then James's preaching is consonant and congruent with the proclamation that we find in the apostle Paul.

The Numerous Old Testament Citations That State, for Example, "I Love Thy Law"

But, "the Law" and "delight in the Law" are two mutually exclusive realities! Pietists use Ps 119 as their premiere argument to establish a third use of the Law. They claim that because the psalmist there delights in the Law, the Law must be a Christian's friend! But Reformation theology teaches that only where there is freedom *from* the Law, and only where the Law has lost its power (which is inherently and essentially threat, wrath, and God's total attack on human sin), can there be any love for the Law. Christians don't love the Law because they are now newly able to keep it. They love the Law *because* it has already been fulfilled for them. Luther writes about Ps 119:

> The entire psalm speaks about Christ and his kingdom and the gospel. Yet Christ is the fulfillment of the Law. When he is present, the Law loses its power. It cannot administer wrath because Christ has freed us from it. Therefore, believers delight in the Law.[4]

Nonintuitively, "the Law" group and "those who love the Law" describe two opposed and distinct realities. The Law group has the Law in front of them to do. For them, they still live in the land of if-then. Those who love the Law have the Law behind them as already done. They live in the land of because-therefore. To say that they love the Law is possible only because it is synonymous with saying that they love Christ. Similarly, when the psalmist says that he loves the Law, he must also literally believe what God's own given name proclaims: "The Lord is our righteousness." (Pss 7:17; 31:1; 35:24; 50:6; 71:2, 16, 19; 97:6; 119:40, 42; 143:1, 11; 145:7; Jer 23:6; 33:16)

Consider, then, the 176 verses of Ps 119, where each verse proclaims its love of "thy Law" or one of its synonyms—thy word, thy testimonies, thy ways, thy precepts, thy statutes, thy commandments, and thy rules. The critical interpretive question is, shall we read and interpret each of these verses to refer narrowly to the Ten Commandments or, rather, to refer to the whole of God's revelation in his word? The Pietist claims that clearly this psalm, in its entirety, refers to the Torah. However, among the synonyms are these inclusions: thy steadfast love, thy promise, thy faithfulness, and your appointment (vv. 41, 50, 58, 64, 76, 82, 84, 90, 116, 123,

---

4. WA 39I:372.19–373.9–10.

133, 148, 149, 154). "Thy steadfast love" cannot be made into a synonym for Torah! So the conclusion must be that this psalm is a paeon of praise for the whole of God's revelation, rather than referring in a restricted and narrow way to Torah.

The core question remains: Is the Law given to prescribe human obedience or, rather, to reveal God's righteous holiness? Surely, Ps 119 addresses obedience. That is not the issue. The issue is whether the Law can produce such obedience. Paul, the biblical scholar, taught by Jesus himself, says, "Absolutely not!" "Do you not hear the law?" he cries out in Gal 4:21. If the Law cannot produce obedience, but merely restrains the beast within each of us, is there some other power that does produce obedience? And there is. These psalm verses assert that this power is the promise of God's gracious election, the assurance of God's faithfulness, and God's steadfast love. These are the only powers that can work such a miracle as willing obedience.

Paul recounts for us the event of the giving of the Law with its attendant terrors to show every human being that the Law was never given to be your friend—that is, a humanly achievable to-do list. The book of Joshua and the entire book of Judges recount four hundred years of recurring failure after failure by *God's people* who, among all the populations of the earth alone, have been given God's Law as their proudest distinction, only to continually fail to achieve even a proximity of continued obedience.

I have never heard a pastor brave enough to preach on these verses from Joshua 24:19–22:

> But Joshua said to the people, "You are not able to serve the LORD, for he is a holy God. He is a jealous God. He will not forgive your transgressions or your sins if you forsake the LORD and serve foreign gods. Then he will turn and do you harm and consume you, after having done you good." And the people said to Joshua, "No, but we will serve the LORD." Then Joshua said to the people, "You are witnesses against yourselves."

So much for the Law's ability to make us good boys and girls.

We turn now to the prophets, skipping over the sad history of the kings of Judah and Israel. Ezekiel 23 recounts the summary of that whole history–God's historical wrath, first against Israel and then against Judah for their "whoring" idolatry. Hosea is asked to marry an unfaithful prostitute in order to proclaim to God's people, in searing human fashion, the anguish God feels in his own heart when his own people chase after every god except him. They trash God's faithfulness. They trash his steadfast love. God cries out,

> What shall I do with you, O Ephraim? What shall I do with you, O Judah? Your love is like a morning cloud; like the dew that goes early away. Therefore, I have hewn them by the prophets; I have slain then by the words of my mouth, and my judgment goes forth as the light. For I desire steadfast love and not sacrifice, the knowledge of God rather than burnt offerings. (Hos 6:4–6)

Significantly, Jesus tells the faculty at Jerusalem, regarding that last verse, to "go and *learn* what this means" (Matt 9:13; italics added). Evidently God is after something other than a humanly achievable to-do list.

God is after a whole new heart. What Jeremiah could not yet see is that this promise of a new heart was going to consist of God himself indwelling us. Jeremiah describes, in God's own words, that coming promise:

> Behold, the days are coming, declares the LORD, when I will make a new covenant with the house of Israel and the house of Judah, not like the covenant that I made with their fathers on the day when I took them by the hand to bring them out of the land of Egypt, my covenant that they broke, though I was their husband, declares the LORD. But this is the covenant that I will make with the house of Israel after those days, declares the LORD: I will put my law within them, and I will write it on their hearts. And I will be their God, and they shall be my people. And no longer shall each one teach his neighbor and each his brother, saying "Know the LORD," for they shall all know me, from the least of them to the greatest, declares the LORD. For I will forgive their iniquity and I will remember their sin no more. (Jer 31:31–34)

Obedience was always in view in the old covenant but never accomplished. Knowing the LORD is the new obedience. Knowing the LORD creates delight and new desires to please him. Because obedience is the rightful and best praise to God that his children can give him.

Nevertheless, the Pietist fears that such obedience will never happen in our new sanctification without the attendant and necessary old covenant Law, together with its threatening punishments. But this is fundamentally rejected by the entire Old Testament witness and by God's own summary word. Both have demonstrated through almost three millennia that the Law, used by its best hearers, never created what only an alien righteousness can achieve. What other people on the planet have ever published such a thorough condemnation of itself? Why would God want us to study this? These millennia of disobedience are not the Law's fault. Paul said it best: the Law is holy, right, good, and eternal. The problem lies in that the Law had nothing to work with, given that we are flesh and sold under sin.

CHAPTER 5

The Foundation for Paul's Argument Regarding the Law

NO SINGLE CHAPTER CAN adequately cover Paul's theology regarding the Law. The following eight headings are meant to act like the red and green buoys that line the edges of American waterways, designed to guide boats safely into the main channel. The following list is meant merely to distill some of the central components of his thought, so that the main point emerges more clearly.

Two Kingdoms

In Rom 5:20–21 one finds the critical foundation for Paul's subsequent argument that extends to the end of chapter 8. Here Paul asserts that only two possible kingdoms exist. Each kingdom is defined by a triad of powers. The first kingdom is labelled *Law-sin-death*. The second is labelled *grace-righteousness-life*. The three terms in each label are exact contrasting correlates of the other.

After the fall, human beings exist only in the first kingdom. Interestingly, Paul argues that the Law part of this kingdom entered only later, even though sin reigned before the Law's arrival with its condemnation (Rom 5:13). Surprisingly, and nonintuitively, the Law was given by God to only make things worse! "So that every mouth may be stopped and the whole world held accountable to God" (Rom 3:19). Its terribly fearful, sole function is diagnostic, and not directive! That is, the Law was given to locate and confirm in you what you deny or hide from, and what you would be unable to see because of sin's blinding effect. It has only one possible report by reason of the weakness of our flesh—"You are sick!" "Therefore no one will be declared righteous in God's sight by observing the law" (Rom 3:20). It defies explanation why and how Pietists refuse to understand that this clear sentence eliminates any possibility of attaining human righteousness! How can Paul say anything more directly than this, that the Law's God-given condemning role is its sole function?

The Law's insistence upon perfection leaves only two possible options: either the Law must die or we must die. Since the Law is holy, eternal, and from heaven, it will not and cannot die. Our only salvation is that we die. We die to the Law! How our death saves us is God's miracle, which Paul now goes on to explain.

The Exodus Crossing

Every Israelite is taught their basic salvation story. It has these basic parts:

1) You were once slaves in Egypt where your only fate was death.

2) God brought you out of Egypt by a savior called Moses, who led you out of slavery and brought you to a miraculous crossing through an ocean of water, which was pushed to the side for your exodus.

3) On the far side of the exodus crossing you looked back at the destruction of your enemies and rejoiced in God's salvation.

4) But, turning forward to the future, you faced a challenging wilderness whose crossing is filled with threatening dangers and personal enemies.

5) On this part of the journey you were faithfully led all the way, not by the Law, but by God's presence in a living pillar of cloud by day and of fire by night.

6) The Law was given, in that wilderness, with frightening display of holiness. And directions for worship and obedience were established.

7) Ahead was the promised land, achieved by another crossing, yet again on dry land, through the river Jordan.

Paul argues that your death with Christ in baptism is your exodus crossing, both here in Rom 6 and also in 1 Cor 10:1–2. You died in your baptism exodus. Only that death could bring to an end your slavery in the land of Law-sin-death. Law still exists and affects the flesh side of you, but cannot reside new-life side. Sin still exists and torments the flesh side of you, but, because by dying you are no longer its slave, for the first time the

Spirit gives you the power to resist its temptations. Our mortality still lies ahead, but Paul says that it has been transformed. Only Christ dies. You have already died with him and so you only "fall asleep" (1 Thess 4:15). We have *already* died! That is our continuing comfort.

Christians need to know their current and historical location. Just as you use shopping mall maps to locate yourself in the mall, the Christian uses the you-are-here map of their own exodus crossing. This map locates you on the far side of the crossing, delivered from the enslaving powers of the old kingdom (items 3 and 4 above). You, as well as the old Israel, share the same exodus pattern.

It is critical, though, to understand what you are exiting from and to. Here the exodus is decidedly *not* the presumed Pietist's exodus from vice to virtue, but rather the scriptural exodus from virtue to *grace*. In this new exodus, Christians are not "every day and in every way"[1] advancing in human righteousness but, rather, leaving all human righteousness behind; they believe more and more in Christ's righteousness. Thus, the exodus *from* virtue, *to* grace. This new exodus is away from virtue, because virtue depends upon the Law. On the far shore of Christianity, a brand new power, other than Law, is in control and has been demonstrated.

Critical to Paul's argument is that *you have died*! (That is the critical component that creates the far side.) It is necessary to what follows, because it is a central fact of our salvation that the Law can get no more work out of a dead slave. But this is precisely what Pietism denies. Pietism must keep the old self alive so that it can become a new and improved version of *human righteousness* through following the Law's guidance (by the power of the Spirit, of course). Instead of this, Paul emphatically states in Gal 2:19–20,

> For through the law *I died* to the law so that I might live for God. I have been crucified with Christ and *I no longer live*, but Christ lives in me. And the life I live in the body, I live by faith in the Son of God who loved me and gave himself for me. (Italics added)

Everywhere his description of this new life is that by faith we have a new, alien righteousness—the righteousness of Christ.

So, then, for Christians, this exodus describes the two historical periods in their lives:

---

1. A phrase coined by French psychologist Émile Coué in the early twentieth century.

- before our connection to the death of Jesus on the cross in holy baptism, and
- after, where we are raised to new life and given the indwelling Spirit.

Christians live no longer in the slavery of the previous Egypt-land of Law-sin-death. Everything in that "before" is controlled by the powers of Law-sin-death. The historical event of our exodus through being joined to the death of Christ brings us into the "after" domain of grace-righteousness-life. The Law cannot jump the fence into that new domain of grace-righteousness-life. That is the whole point. The central argument of Rom 6, 7, and 8 is that the Law never could produce virtue (human righteousness). Therefore, the Law cannot be permitted to belong in any conversation regarding the new life, or the new obedience founded on faith in Christ. The Law is unnecessary there because the Holy Spirit is the new director and motivator. The Law, reintroduced there, will annihilate our Christian freedom (Gal 5:1). The continuing use of the Law for a Christian is limited to its power to expose sin and therefore to drive us to Christ (the second use).

Living in the Land of *If-Then* Versus the Land of *Because-Therefore*

The most definitive evidence that one is still enslaved under the powers of the kingdom of Law-sin-death is revealed by one's use of the only possible vocabulary in that land: *if-then*. Having taught confirmation classes to junior high students for many decades, I can attest to the fact that if-then is the only kingdom that seventh and eighth graders understand. The Law-land of if-then is the only world they have experienced and have learned to navigate. They are past masters of the Law, and cannot imagine that there even exists any another world or operating system. Literally the first question from any class is some form of "What will happen to me *if* I don't do my assignment? What will you do to me *then*? Will you call my parents?" et cetera, et cetera, et cetera. If-then, if-then—this is the land of Law. The vocabulary of the land of the Law includes phrases like "You need to," "You must," "You should," "Unless you." These phrases contrast to the vocabulary of the land of grace and faith, which is the land of because-therefore. This land includes contrasting phrases of the new obedience such as this: "In Christ, you have," "Rejoice," "Give thanks always."

Instead of "You need to" or "You must," Paul preaches four whole chapters in 2 Cor 3–6 with eight paragraph headings titled "We Have"!

- We have *confidence* through Christ toward God! (3:4)
- We have such a *hope*! (3:12)
- We have this *ministry*! (4:1)
- We have this *treasure* in earthen vessels! (4:7)
- We have the same *spirit of faith*! (4:13)
- We have a *building* from God . . . eternal in the heavens! (5:1)
- We possess *everything*! (6:10)
- We have these *promises*! (7:1)

The land of because-therefore provides an utter contrast to the innumerable set of anguished demands from the land of if-then. Because-therefore is the vocabulary from the land where there is no Law at all! No Law at all? That phrase alone drives Pietists crazy. The reason that there does not need to be any Law at all is because everything that the Law only dreamed about but never could produce is already yours, and already accomplished! *Because* of this, *therefore* we enjoy the sevenfold fruit of the Spirit—love, joy, peace, patience, kindness, goodness, faithfulness, gentleness, and self control—all of which come as a package. Christ has already fulfilled what is impossible for you—the twofold summary command of the Law "Love God with all your heart" and "Love your neighbor as yourself" (Matt 22:37-39; Mark 12:30-31; Luke 10:27). Since this is already done for you by Another, the Law has absolutely nothing left to say to you. As Luther proclaims, "The Law says, 'Do this!' and it is never done. In contrast, the gospel says, "Do this" and it is 'Already done!'"[2] To the Pietists who incessantly worry that without the Law, we will misbehave, Paul says in Gal 5:16–17,

> So I say, live by the Spirit and you will not gratify the desires of the sinful nature. The desires of the flesh are against the Spirit, and the desires of the Spirit are against the flesh, for these are opposed to each other to prevent you from doing what you would.

---

2. See appendix II, thesis 26.

Related closely to the because-therefore thought world of the gospel of Paul is his recurring phrase describing the ongoing contrast between flesh and Spirit. Though both powers reside within every Christian, in unending mortal conflict with each other, nevertheless Paul constantly says, "Once you were," but "Now you are" (Eph 2:11–22).

Flesh and Spirit, the Plight of the "I"

Romans 7, arguably the single most fought over chapter in the New Testament, has interpretive proponents on each of two unalterably opposed sides. On one side, the Pietists hold that Paul, if he is here *describing his existence as a Christian*, could not have said, "For I know that nothing good dwells in me, that is in my flesh. For I have the desire to do what is right, but not the ability to carry it out. For I do not do the good I want, but the evil I do not want is what I keep on doing" (Rom 7:18–19). Therefore, these interpreters insist that, in those words, Paul is describing himself *before* he became a Christian. All Pietists insist that these words only make sense describing his life as a *pre-Christian*.

The other (and minority) side interprets these verses as a most robust and accurate description of a Christian who is still inhabited by the temptations and inability of the flesh. Here, the plight of the new "I" is described by the suffering with which faith has to contend. While Christians believe that we have been made completely righteous in Christ, and remain so every moment, the problem is that we cannot with any of our senses apprehend or detect that this is so. At the same time, in every moment of our existence, all of our senses together are screaming at us the very opposite, that we are empirically and demonstrably unrighteous. And so we live by faith alone that we are righteous.

What inevitably follows is that we have two unalterably opposed solutions to the plight of the "I" so described. First, there is the Pietist solution: "I am no longer that person! I can now produce real human righteousness through a newly able obedience, using the Holy Spirit's power." But this is the old analog (partial but never complete) solution where the goal is never achievable. Because of the partial nature of this human righteousness, the medieval church had a whole industry of actions to get one from one's baptism to the finish line of salvation. There had to be prescribed penances, indulgences, and special masses to be said to abbreviate one's time in purgatory. Assurance of faith was assumed to be impossible. "But surely God is merciful" etc. But how is the Pietist position essentially different that this?

In contrast to all this is the alternate Pauline and Lutheran solution: You never could, and you never will, be able to be humanly righteous! Therefore, cling to the faith that you have a complete righteousness, not your own, but that which belongs to Christ, who has already completed it. This produces the rare biblical (and uniquely Lutheran) description, that a Christian is both 100 percent sinner and 100 percent righteous, *at the same time, all the time*. Righteousness then becomes a 100 percent state, like pregnancy. One cannot be 85 percent pregnant. Righteousness, according to Paul, is never analog. Christian righteousness is all or nothing. The "all" of Christ's righteousness is God's total attack on sin.

This means that the Christian *body* becomes the battlefield between two mortally and implacably opposed foes, flesh and Spirit. Since we will never be free from the continuing influence of the power of the flesh until our resurrection, our salvation can be described quite accurately as an on-going, never completed, exorcism. The Holy Spirit opposes the flesh to prevent us from doing what we would. Yes, we make progress. But not as the world expects. Our progress is more like regress. A Christian only "progresses" in the appalling and growing recognition regarding how much we need grace. The office of the Holy Spirit is to move ever deeper within, to gradually reveal to us, in growing detail, the extent of the sin we have failed to recognize. The progress consists of the growing recognition of how much we need, and are supported by, amazing grace. A Lutheran missionary from Madagascar, Professor Duane Olson, described this in a way that not a single one of my church members has so far understood. He said, "A Christian grows like the tail of a cow—downward."[3] Christian "progress" is downward, as this progress takes the shape of increasing humility and awe, before such a gracious God.

Works or Faith

> We hold that one is justified by faith *apart* from works of the law. (Rom 3:28; italics added)
>
> Israel who pursued a law that would lead to righteousness did not succeed in reaching that law. Why? *Because they did not*

---

3. From an unpublished sermon.

> *pursue it by faith, but as if it were based on works.* (Rom 9:32; italics added)

Everything that does not come from faith is sin. (Rom 14:23)

In verse 28 above, the word "apart" (*xoris* in Greek[4]) is emphatic. It denotes an absolute separation, with no possible relation between the two terms. Why the apostle Paul makes the nonintuitive and absolute contrast between faith and works demands careful consideration. Most essentially, it involves which *agency* gets to define what constitutes a "good work." According to Pietists, there has to be an objective standard for whether an action is good or bad, which, in turn, has to be adjudicated by the empirical standard of the Law, or else proper ethics becomes impossible! But against that argument, it is also clear that the Law was never able to define what constituted a good work because of its inability to discern the right motive, or the right heart, behind the action. Approximation under the Law is not only useless, but damnable.

Paul's argument is that whatever is done in faith is a good work. In addition, all actions of faith are done within the kingdom of grace-righteousness-life, where there is no Law. Therefore, these actions are judged by a different agent and standard than Law. Faith alone makes a work good. In addition, it can be asserted that the Law never was the determinative factor to judge between that which was righteous and that which was not. The Law, in the end, is unable to provide the empirical standard for righteousness that Pietists demand for their ethics. The only biblically determinative factor is whether a deed was done in faith. That is, believing that, because my whole life is lived within the righteousness of Jesus, that action is *counted* as righteous.

Every Christian will face, at some time in their life, a situation where no decision is a good decision. In the novel *Les Miserables*, Victor Hugo gives this example. A priest who has never lied in his life is asked by the pursuing police officer if Jean Valjean has stolen the church's silver candlesticks found in Jean's possession. The priest is faced with two choices, neither of them without sin: (a) tell the police officer that this is so, but then send Jean back to the slave galleys, or (b) lie and say that he gave them to Jean. In the story the priest chose the latter, sinning mercifully.[5] This is a clear illustration of the proper way to understand the sense of Luther's much maligned remark, "Sin boldly, but believe more

---

4. BAGD, s.v. "χωρίς."
5. Hugo, *Les Miserables*, ch. 1.

boldly still!"[6] It is also an illustration of how a Christian lives in actual faith, sometimes without any indication of what is right, yet confident that since we have (and need) a righteousness not our own, God will count our actions mercifully as done in Christ.

Faith hears the word of the Law with completely new ears—no longer as an if-then proposition, but rather as a because-therefore, fulfilled-in-Christ proposition. The Law drives one to faith in Jesus, and thus one arrives at the proper venue of God's blessing. Faith alone, and not Law, creates work that is good in God's sight. "Without faith it is impossible to please him" (Heb 11:6).

Evidently this is what Paul means when he sums up the problem of correctly interpreting the purpose of the Law in the whole Old Testament narrative when he writes, "Because they did not pursue it [righteousness] by faith, but as if it were based on works" (Rom 9:32). Surely obedience is in view here. But what *was* the content of the Old Testament faith to produce that obedience, since Christ had not yet appeared?

The content of Israel's faith (and thus, its obedience) was based upon two God-revealed things. The first was the promise. Abraham believed God's promise, and it was reckoned to him as righteousness. That promise extended to each descendant of Abraham, to each person of the nation of Israel. The promise took the form of the central word to Israel's faith and theology—*chesed*—being "chosen by God" to be forever surrounded by his faithful love. The second God-revealed foundation for the faith of Israel is the repeated gospel claim found everywhere in the Old Testament revelation—the name of God himself—"the Lord is our righteousness." A partial list of the Psalms identifying their rescue on the basis of the Lord's righteousness, or upon the Lord's righteous judgments, or upon faith in his righteousness providing the foundation for all things, can be found in the following citations: Pss 7:17; 9:8; 31;1; 35:24, 28; 36:6; 50:6; 71:2, 16, 19; 72:1–3; 89:16; 96:13; 97:2, 6; 98:9; 99:4; 103:17; 111:3; 112:3, 9; 118:19; 119:40, 42; 143:1; and 145:7. The Prophets take up this theme that the Lord is our righteousness in Isa 5:16; 11:4–5; 28:17; 42:6; 57:12; 58:8; 59:16–17; Jer 23:6; 33:16; Ezek 33:12–18; Zech 8:8; and Mal 4:2. One of their kings was even named Zedekiah—"the Lord is our righteousness." How strange, then, that *that* name and promise of God so rarely appears in any current preaching, on either of the Testaments!

---

6. *LW* 48:281–82.

It is very revealing to note that, related to the faith-works contrast, church fathers before Luther spent far more time on love than upon faith. If they talked about faith at all, faith was only valid if faith was formed by love. This scholastic dogma had two hideous errors. First, since love is the fulfilling of the Law, and since Law was understood to define which works were good, this "formed by love" formulation was secretly all about attaining human righteousness through the Law. Insisting upon the human empirical standard of rules, rather than jettisoning human righteousness completely, is the primary human defense mechanism against having to rely 100 percent upon the righteousness of Jesus (cf. Phil 3:1–9). Second, this scholastic theology was self-defeating, since the Law can never produce the love that it commands. "Did you receive the Spirit by works of the law or by hearing with faith?" Paul asks (Gal 3:2). "Do you not hear the law?" he shouts (Gal 4:21). "Now it is evident that no one is justified before God by the law, for, 'The righteous shall live by faith'" (Gal 3:11). In short, scripturally, it is faith versus the Law and never as a combination. Christian ethics are run by faith alone!

The Problem of Two Laws

"For the law of the Spirit of life has set you free in Christ Jesus from the law of sin and death" (Rom 8:2). It is confusing that Paul uses *law* in two ways. First, Paul uses law as the condemning power of a heaven-sent command (which I have capitalized as *Law* throughout this book). But then he also uses the same term in the phrase "the law of the Spirit of life" as the functioning power of the new covenant. Pietists fail to make the distinction between these two *laws*, insisting that there is only one Law. They do the same when it comes to phrases like "the law of Christ."

Out of the 375 times Paul uses the name *Christ* in his thirteen letters, and out of the 129 times he uses the term *law* in the same letters, the phrase "the law of Christ" shows up exactly *once*. In 1 Cor 9:19–21 we read the relevant argument:

> For though I am free from all men, I have made myself a slave to all, that I might win the more. To the Jews I became as a Jew, in order to win Jews; to those under the law I become as one under the law—though not being myself under the law—that I might win those under the law. To those outside the law I became as one outside the law—not being without law toward God but

under the *law of Christ*—that I might win those outside the law. (Italics added.)

It is very clear here that, contrary to Pietist teaching, Paul does not equate the Law of Christ with the Law of the decalogue. In fact, he is carefully and deliberately making the contrast between the two!

In the Gospel of John and in his epistles, John makes a distinction between the terms *Law* and *commandment*. In John 7 Jesus takes on the Jerusalem faculty in a devastating discussion summarized by Jesus accusing them, "Yet none of you keeps the law" (v. 19). Then, in chapter 13:34 and in chapter 15:12, where we hear about the Holy Spirit, we hear about a "new commandment." This newness cannot be the same as the old Law, but must have a new agent—the Holy Spirit—who alone can enable such a miracle as this: "To love one another as I have loved you." So this new commandment is in no way related to the Law but, rather, fulfills that which the Law could only prescribe but never accomplish. In 1 John 2:8 we hear that this new commandment "is true in him and in you." In 3:23 we hear that this new commandment is that "we believe in the name of his Son, Jesus Christ, and love one another." In 4:19 we hear that "we love because he first loved us." And in 2 John 1:6 we hear that "you follow love."

In summary, we learn that biblically there are two distinct powers engaged in the life of a Christian. The first is the Law, whose God-given function is limited to exposing sin, accusing, condemning, terrifying, and killing. "The sting of death is sin, and the power of sin is the law" (1 Cor 15:56). In contrast to this Law is the advent of the Holy Spirit, who *gives* the Law of Christ's righteousness, and whose power brings life and resurrection to formerly dead slaves. One Law is always *demand*. The "law of the Spirit of Christ," the "law of Christ," or the "new commandment" all refer to sheer *gift*.

On Being Conformed to Christ

It is Paul's constant procedure in his letters to write a summary of every major argument in the paragraph title and opening. So, in Rom 12:2 we read the following statement as a summary and title to the Christian answer to all ethics:

> Do not be conformed to this world but be transformed by the renewal of your mind, that by testing you may discern what is the will of God, what is good and acceptable and perfect.

The key word here is "transformed" (from the Greek *metamorphothe*) from which we get the English metamorphosis.[7] The Christian image of this is that of a butterfly emerging winged and beautiful after the metamorphosis from a mere worm. If that metamorphosis is such a miracle, then human transformation and being made to conform to Christ *has* to be God's miracle alone. Previously Paul has said that "those whom he foreknew he also predestined to be conformed to the image of his Son" (Rom 8:29), and he also writes "I am in travail until Christ be formed in you!" (Gal 4:19).

Christocentric conformity can never be an imitation or an act of human will. It has nothing whatever to do with the direction of the Law! To be made to conform to the image of Christ is to be brought, through inner conflict, to die to oneself. To hear and justify God's accusation upon us is terrifying. Here one becomes completely helpless, *so that* one can experience God's faithful power. The experience of human inability is so terrifying, that Pietists introduce the concept of cheap grace. The Pietists' offered solution to avoid making God's offer of grace cheap is for us to find a confidence in the Law's ability to use grace properly. With it, we *try harder to keep the Law*. The Pietist solution has at least two flaws. First, it falsely believes that human improvement through the Holy Spirit enables one to redefine keeping the Law *to mere improvement*, because Christ has covered the rest. Second, it falsely believes that the Law has the continuing power to direct us in holiness, while falsely refusing to believe in the power of God's grace alone to transform.

Once again, the Law mocks all human attempt. It is the proper hearing of the Law together with its killing revelation that you are helpless, that is the real solution to cheap grace. Only the Holy Spirit can take us through this dying to oneself. This helpless dying is so terrifying at times as to require God's miracle of faith to survive it. Inner conflict is not only normal, but essential in this conforming process. This suffering is *the* most essential indication that we are really God's own children, as we hear in Rom 8:16. We are constantly being put to death so that we can live. Only the Holy Spirit can help us stand up in this gracious killing.

---

7. BAGD, s.v. "μεταμορφόω."

Being conformed to Christ is painful and terrifying. But God's way for you is the same as the way Christ took—through death to life.

Another critical component to this transformation needs to be discussed. Conformity to Christ and the concept of the good are inextricably related.

To repeat what was said earlier, the good is no simple thing! When Adam and Eve were tempted by the serpent with the promise that they would "be like God, knowing good and evil," they listened to him and ate of the forbidden fruit. When their eyes were opened, they did know evil. But, terrifyingly, they found themselves cut off from the good. They now knew that there was *a* good, but since God alone determined the good, and they were now away from God, they no longer were able to know what the good was! Completely cut off from access to the good, they were inevitably forced into the position of trying to approximate the good. But this very attempt to approximate the good *is* the essential original sin of attempting to be like God. Worse, it is not only hopeless, it is damnable. It is deeply instructive to watch the judiciary of the United States (merely at the level of civil law) flail, tilt at, and continually fight over conflicting definitions of the good. Again, enter any law office to see the endless hundreds of volumes making up case law. All this demonstrates the utter futility of the human pursuit to hopefully approximate the good. Our endless effort to, by the Law, discover some definitive definition of the good is a futile and damnable project seeking to make us like God. This is the original sin.

In the Scripture, we fast forward now to the giving of the Law at Sinai, which according to Paul only makes matters worse! The sole and singular function of the Law is to reveal to humans that which is not the good. The Law heard properly is like the familiar street signs that helpfully say "No Exit" or "Dead End." These signs are ostensive. That is, they point away from themselves and require of us another direction. What that particular direction is, however, these signs are unable to say. In exactly the same way, and not by approximate metaphor, the Law reveals to us that the only correct venue is *away* from the not good. But any other direction than this is not to be found in the Law! Additionally, the Law shuts down, by its impossible demands, any human attempt to approximate, let alone achieve the good. Nevertheless, humans constantly design endless attempts to satisfy our longing to be good, because our hearts condemn us (Rom 2:1–3).

The various attempts to do so include the entire field of ethics, all attempts at moralism, idealistic philosophy, and, most essentially, the Pietist attempt to use the Law to define, determine, or find the correct direction to locate and perform the good. However, the Law is only ostensive. It says, "I don't have the answer. If you want the answer, go to Jesus." When that happens, then the Law's job is done, and its voice is no longer necessary. Both Paul and Luther insist upon that point.

Proud reason and the empirical method are hopeless here, for the same basic reason realized by Adam and Eve when their eyes were opened. Neither reason nor the empirical method are able to create communion with God. Those who ridicule Christians who fail to believe in empirical standards of righteousness measurable or evident by some Law method only reveal the fear of the abject failure of their own method. Nevertheless, because Christian faith fails every test or measurement by reason or the empirical method, the opposition calls us lawless or antinomian.

Utterly foundational in this argument is that *only God can define and perform that which is the good*. And that leads us back to being *conformed to Christ*. "It is no longer I who live, but Christ who lives in me" says Paul in Gal 2:20. Precisely! If so, then any good work done by a Christian is done by Christ who dwells within. All human righteousness is, and has, by this definition, to be ruled out. The resulting works of Christ flow spontaneously out of a Christian believer. These works reveal themselves in the person who believes what the Law was sent to do—"That every mouth may be stopped and the whole *world* held accountable to God. For by works of the law no human being will be justified in his sight, since through the law comes the knowledge of sin" (Rom 3:19–20; italics added). Only Christians *agree* with this judgment of God! Every single other person in the world fights against this judgment in some way. Only the Christian comes to know that God's love comes with judgment: a Christian who, in hearing God's fearful judgment against his sin, simply says, "It is the Lord," and humbly submits.

But in the midst of the Christian submitting, a joyful surprise happens. God's faithful love is miraculously shown and experienced in the heart. So, only Christians come to believe in the massive words "But now" that follow the summary judgment of Rom 3:19–20. And *now*, by faith, Christians lean on the alien and complete righteousness of Christ revealed in verses 22–26. There, we are saved by the righteousness *of* Jesus. Critically, this is not the mistranslated "saved by our faith *in* the righteousness of Jesus" (so also in the ESV rendition; italics added). The change of agents implied in these two competing renditions of Paul's most distilled thesis is critically important, because the faith *of* Jesus is what constitutes and defines our new imputed righteousness. Jesus's goodness is the only sure foundation for proper Christian assurance.

The Holy Spirit, who creates this faith, is the real presence of God. He is the mediator of the real presence of Christ. The contrast between flesh and Spirit in Paul's writing is the contrast between the whole person without the real presence of God, and the whole of a person within and under this real presence of God.[8]

Suffering under the Holy Spirit's work of conforming us to Christ means jettisoning all human attempts at works in favor of faith in the righteousness of Christ alone. Works encompasses and includes every human effort to approximate the good:

- whether it attempts to use the Law as a false prescriptive to locate the good,
- whether it attempts to use reason,
- whether it attempts to use empirical method,
- whether it attempts to use moralism,
- whether it attempts to use idealism, or
- whether it attempts to use any system of ethics.

Paul asks, "Do we then overthrow the law by this faith? By no means! On the contrary, we uphold the law" (Rom 3:31). How? By answering the only possible solution to the Law's ostensive direction, away from itself, to Christ, who is the only content of the good.

Jesus's Organic Righteousness

> Filled with the fruit of righteousness, *that comes through Jesus Christ*. (Phil 1:11; italics added)

> Abide in me and I in you. As the branch cannot bear fruit by itself, unless it abides in the vine, neither can you, unless you abide in me. (John 15:4)

---

8. Prenter, *Spiritus Creator*, 26.

Note above that saving righteousness flows from Jesus, and not from ourselves. Left to ourselves, we will always seek to perform righteousness according to the Law. But according to the very succinct scripture above, all saving righteousness flows from Jesus *alone* (*sola*). It has nothing to do with our cooperation or participation. Righteousness does not flow from the Law! What flows from the Law is only condemnation. Yet that fearful condemnation is a God-given mercy, so that we will look elsewhere. By the Law's inescapable accusation against us, we are pointed to Jesus alone.

So then, any attempt to perform our own righteousness only hinders the Holy Spirit's production of Jesus's righteousness and new obedience in a Christian. Since those attempts always only hinder the production of the righteousness counted to us by trusting the faith of Jesus, how is there any room left for a third use of the Law?

If Jesus's righteousness is a fruit, it is *organic*. Organic means that you do not know how it happens! You only know that it *does*. So, if one does not (and cannot) know how this new righteousness happens, obviously the Law's direction is of no use.

Finally, the Law is of no empirical use to determine what is, and what is not, a good work. If righteousness belongs to Jesus alone, then the original sin is our everlasting attempt to approximate a good work, by our own understanding, rather than trusting Jesus to produce his work in us. This indicates that the vital contrast defining the only possibility of Christian ethics is between the sure confidence and faith that Jesus's righteousness belongs to us, versus the misapprehension that the Law's given function is to direct or define that righteousness. However, Scripture is adamant: faith remains the *only* functional power to direct us into godliness.

Summary

In order to demonstrate that Paul's proclamation of the gospel holds only an apparently dangerous position regarding Law, it is necessary clearly to understand these component parts of his description of the new reality we have been given in Christ.

- First, the arrival of the new kingdom of *grace-righteousness-life* absolutely excludes the old triumvirate powers of *Law-sin-death*. Each kingdom completely annihilates the other. The two cannot possibly be combined. For that reason, Law can be allowed no place in

Christ's new kingdom, especially in its call to a new "walk by the Spirit" (Gal 5:16). A Christian lives under a new power, not under the Law.

- Second, the exodus *from* virtue *to* grace is the exodus from Law and its moralism, casuistry, idealism, and its trust in the possible "improvement" of our flesh.
- Third, that exodus is by our dying with Christ in baptism. This creates two periods of history in a Christian life, the new period being a resurrected life in which the Law can no longer torture a dead slave.
- Fourth, while the Law implicitly insists upon the apprehension of the new life by means of renewed human ability, the coming of faith stands completely against that. Since the righteousness of Christ is not apparent to any of the five senses, the righteousness of Christ is apprehended by faith alone and is not apparent to the believer. This, again, excludes the Law's insistence upon its evidentiary empiricism.
- Fifth, devastatingly, the Law offers no hope of success in its endlessly futile attempts to approximate the good.
- Sixth, since the good is spiritual, and spiritually apprehended, and the five senses cannot apprehend the good, the Holy Spirit must reveal it. In Rom 12:2, Paul calls this Holy Spirit transformation "the new mind." Luther understands this venue as the renewed conscience, which we will discuss in a subsequent chapter. Only the new mind receives what the Holy Spirit gives, by faith.
- Finally, the righteousness of faith is a *fruit* that comes through Jesus. Fruit is organic. That means that it lives and exists beyond empirical explanation. Nevertheless, it is empirically evident and real.

Chapter 6

The Third Use of the Law in the Light of Good Friday and Easter

Consider, first, what is happening on Good Friday under the kingdom powers of Law-sin-death.

- "God made him to be *sin* who knew no sin, so that we could be the righteousness of God" (2 Cor 5:21; italics added). So, according to Scripture, *all* sin was laid in one place, on Jesus's shoulders at the cross.
- It then follows that the *Law* asserts its right by God's own decree, "The soul that sins shall die" (Ezek 18:4), and rightly claims its victim.
- At Jesus's *death*, in his dying he cries out, certainly referring to all these three powers, "It is finished!" (John 19:30).

Now consider Easter morning.

- Where is *sin*? If there were just one sin unatoned, the Law could have said to Jesus, "Not so fast! I still have you by right!" But that did not happen. So logically, we have implicit proof that *all* sin is buried and gone.
- Where is *death*? Jesus is alive, and his new body is no longer touchable by death. His new body, as in the previous case, is standing testimony that sin is forever buried.
- Where is *Law*? It has vanished. Why? Because all its claims have been satisfied in the one Righteous One—the New Man. The vision for every Christian on Easter Day is no sin, no death, no Law, but only grace, righteousness, and life. Paul proclaims in Rom 6 that this not only was done for you but that it belongs completely to all who

have been baptized! Your baptism connects you to Christ's death so that real life could arise. You are also raised with him to walk in a new life, as the new humanity.

Summary: On Good Friday, the Law-sin-death triumvirate was in darkness swirling around and triumphant. On Easter Day, filled with light, *none of them* are evident any longer. All who are connected to this event through baptism have been raised from death, to walk a new life.

In contrast to this, the third-users group try to keep the old man deathless, so as not to go through the killing that is necessary for the new to arise. In response to Augustine's attacks, Pelagius insists that *grace* means the natural capacities God created in humans, especially the free choice of the will, or, in the case of the third use of the Law, how to live by our new spiritual powers from the Holy Spirit.[1] Voila! Grace suddenly changes the critical agency affecting salvation from God to man! This redefinition of grace makes salvation into a human righteousness project rendering help from God or the cross of Christ as merely ancillary. This did not prove difficult to refute, using only basic biblical witness. Moreover, as Luther later pointed out, two marvelous ironies develop here, demonstrating that this theology is almost comical. First, the Law, which is spoken by God to *kill*, is used by Pelagius as a vehicle to achieve *life*! But this refutes Paul's whole argument in Galatians, where he clearly states the there was never, ever, a law given that could give life (Gal 2:16; 3:21; 5:1–4). Second, instead of the gospel resurrecting and creating a whole new person, it is used to be a crutch for the *dying person*! And so, as Luther said in the Heidelberg Disputation, "Without the cross, man uses the best things in the worst way."[2]

Paul continues with the baptism argument that it is all apprehended by faith. It is by faith that we lean into our only hope: life that is finally and definitively freed from slavery and terror under the kingdom of Law-sin-death by coming under the new aegis of grace-righteousness-life. Here *faith* is almost synonymous with Jesus. In Gal 3:23–25 we read that "faith came," "Jesus came," "faith came," showing that faith is not a volitional concept but rather a miraculous gift to whomever God pleases. This new confidence brims with love, joy, and peace.

Grace is also defined as Jesus's righteousness. The entire content of grace is Jesus's righteousness! "But now the righteousness of God

---

1. In Augustine, *On Nature and Grace*.
2. See appendix II, thesis 24.

has been revealed, the righteousness *of* Jesus, for all who believe" (Rom 3:21–22; italics added). As noted previously, this same careful, dense thesis statement is repeated almost verbatim in Gal 2:16 and Phil 3:9, demonstrating that this formulation is no accidental expression but is rather foundational to all Paul's preaching. A footnote is necessary in each of these citations because the majority of modern translators, including the Calvinist translators of the English Standard Version used in this book, choose to render this verse that our faith *in* Jesus saves us, thus changing the agent from God to us, and making it more in line with current mainstream theology. However, Paul's Greek clearly uses the possessive and not the dative preposition in each of these scriptural citations. Though the possessive case is not the easiest reading, a basic rule of translation is to choose the more difficult reading as the more accurate, because previous translators would seek to smooth things out. The righteousness *of* Jesus is also chosen by the King James Version.

Finally, *life* is only possible where there is no Law left to condemn my remaining fleshly self. In the courtroom of Law there are only two possible verdicts: guilty or innocent. Since all Christians still remain in the flesh, and since we therefore have no possible claim to innocence, some new verdict has, of necessity, to be created for our very survival. And God provides it: "There is now no condemnation for those who are in Christ Jesus" (Rom 8:1)!

But this new verdict of salvation is not possible under the third use of the Law, because under that system the Law remains forever. If it remains even as a "helpful director in the new life," the Law's rightful and just claim over us also remains: if not perfect, then you are *guilty*! The Law is a total claimant. It results always in death. Grace is also a total claimant. Just as the Law was sent by God to be the final attack upon our sin, so also Jesus is sent to be the final and unassailable rescue for those so condemned. The verdict "No condemnation" is only possible because of Jesus's total righteousness, unlike our everlasting partial human achievement. Justification is a total concept just like pregnancy. One cannot be 85 percent pregnant!

However, this continuing declaration by God, over you his child, cannot be apprehended by any of our five senses. We cannot even depend upon fleeting feelings that this is so. We are limited to hearing this good news, over and over again, hanging onto the word alone, to combat the nonending accusation of the Law that we are and remain sinners. So faith is suffering (Rom 5:1–5). But the Holy Spirit, who created the faith in us that Jesus is our righteousness, will also maintain this faith in us and he will carry us safely to the end. He "strengthens and keeps us steadfast in His Word and in faith unto our end. This is His gracious and good will," says Luther in his explanation of the phrase "Thy will be done" in the Lord's Prayer (Matt 6:10).[3]

---

3. Luther, "3rd Petition," 11.

Chapter 7

Five Case Studies Demonstrating the Viability of Paul's Law-Free Ethics

"Imitate Me"

- "And you became imitators of us and of the Lord, for you received the word in much affliction" (1 Thess 1:6).
- "For you yourselves know how you ought to imitate us; we were not idle when we were with you" (2 Thess 3:7).
- "I became your father in Christ Jesus through the gospel. I urge you, then, be imitators of me" (1 Cor 4:15–16).
- "Be imitators of me, as I am of Christ" (1 Cor 11:1).
- "Brethren, join in imitating me, and mark those who so live as you have an example in us" (Phil 3:17).
- "What you have learned, and received, and heard, and seen in me, do; and the God of peace will be with you" (Phil 4:9).

THE NEW ETHICAL STANDARD for Christian behavior, laid out in all of Paul's letters, is organic, Holy Spirit–inspired, and exampled in *persons* (that is, Paul himself, including his helpers such as Timothy). Paul's personal behavior in and with his new congregations is the standard. It is no longer the Law. This is shocking, not just to prospective Christians, but to all human wisdom since.

In the last Philippians citation above, we are asked to imagine what that personal example might consist of. Paul lists two bases for personal evaluation of himself: word and action. "Learned," "received," and "heard" all vitally refer to the preached scriptural word. So mere subjectivity in Christian ethics is here ruled out. What is new is the replacement of the Law by something more organic and Holy Spirit–inspired. One can also observe and follow actions in another, which is made possible in that person by an agent who is different, in kind, than the Law.

To believe in the possibility of such specificity from such person-modeled ethics requires faith that Jesus Christ is present and able to produce measurable actions that more than fulfill the old Law's demands.

Faith in Christ's righteousness via the Holy Spirit's work, and its absolute contrast to human righteousness with its attempt to fulfill the Law, is on the docket here. In bitter and mocking argument, all human righteousness programs simply have to insist upon a codified Law standard. This is because that is the only way to keep ethics in human hands and in human control. In addition, this standard is an attempt to avoid the danger of subjectivity by providing an empirical (and therefore "objective") single standard upon which behavior can be measured and tested. This insistence becomes nonnegotiable, because, arguably, the loss of any objective standard would lead to a hopeless morass of subjectivity where "my truth" trumps "your truth." Thus, all standards for human behavior would disappear. Additionally, it is clear that freedom from the Law, such as Paul preaches (or any freedom, for that matter), can be abused and trampled upon. What a surprise! But Pietists fear this above all else. They believe that without the Law's continued direction Christians will inevitably fall into disobedience.

Those Who Are Weak and Those Who Are Strong in Faith

Paul navigates that precise and valid fear in Rom 14 and 15. He does not yield an inch to scoffers who contend that objectivity is the absolute requirement for any viable ethical program. The first and critical question in any ethics is, "What constitutes a good work?" The Law never was able to make such a determination, because it lacked the ability to discern the motive in the heart of the doer of the action. Therefore, the claim that the Law ever was able to deliver objectivity is a charade and a false, fear-based human claim.

So, if the false claim that only Law delivers objectivity is removed, that still leaves the evident problem that there needs to be some objective definition of what constitutes the truth. Is there no objective and established truth content to which one can appeal?

Evidently not. "I know, and am persuaded in the Lord Jesus, that nothing is unclean in itself, but it is unclean for anyone who thinks it unclean" (Rom 14:14). Clearly stated here is that what is righteous for a Christian who is strong in faith is sin for a Christian who is weak in faith! If that is so, then my truth trumps your truth. And Paul unapologetically acknowledges that this is so.

The reason for this is that faith is now the supreme arbiter and the sole definer of what constitutes a good work. And that changes everything. The Law has always been useless in this respect. The Law's determination of what constitutes righteousness has been definitively redefined by a new determination—was such action done in faith?

An example of this occurred in my first and very rural parish in Montana, located seventeen miles from any paved road. Garbage pickup was not a weekly affair. One of the farmers noted that my garbage container had some beer bottles in it. This offended his sensibilities, together with his belief that all drinking was questionable. If that was so, pastors certainly should not drink! He was a church council member. I was informed of his concern. At the next council meeting I addressed it, assuring him that I would not be drinking any alcohol if that in any way impeded his hearing of the gospel from me. He responded that it was not his right to make such a demand of me. And so the matter was partially resolved Christianly. That is, by the strong seeking to bear with the remaining weaknesses of the weak.

In Pauline ethics, no matter how weak the current faith of some Christians, it is to be respected by those who are strong in faith. However, there is a logical limit to this forbearance. Otherwise, all church actions would be determined by the few persons who say, "That offends me." On the other hand, there is also a logical limit to the church being controlled by only the strong. They would be causing the weak to do that which is still sin for them. "So do not let what is good to you be spoken of as evil. . . . It is right not to eat meat or drink wine or do anything that makes your brother stumble" (Rom 14:16, 21).

Paul's solution places the heavier responsibility upon the strong. "We who are strong ought to bear with the failings of the weak, and not to please ourselves" (15:1). And to all, Paul says, "Welcome one another, therefore, as Christ has taken you to himself, for the glory of God" (15:7). Completely absent here is any appeal to the Ten Commandments or to any other Law.

Human righteousness is all about works. The new Christian righteousness, by contrast, is all about deeds done, freely, by faith in Christ's righteousness. That is why Paul everywhere makes the contrast between faith and works.

Paul's Corinthian Demonstration of Law-Free Ethics

He begins his defense of the possibility of Christian "Law-free" ethics by quoting his (accurate) scoffers, in two different places:

- "'All things are lawful for me,' *but not all things are helpful*. 'All things are lawful for me,' *but I will not be enslaved by anything*" (1 Cor 6:12; italics added).

- "'All things are lawful,' *but not all things are helpful*. 'All things are lawful,' *but not all things build up*" (1 Cor 10:23; italics added).

Paul does not dispute that he is being correctly heard. He cites the exact accusation *so as to refute the false conclusion that Law-free ethics inevitably will lead to anarchy*. Of course Christian freedom can be abused! Of course that is guaranteed to happen! But that is not the critical point. The point is the very viability of the new ethics.

Paul does two things here. First, he articulates the basis for a Christian's new freedom that we hear about most clearly in Gal 5. But he also articulates the inevitable result of Rom 5:20, which required the absolute separation, and the antagonism, between the kingdom of Law-sin-death and the kingdom of grace-righteousness-life. In Rom 5–8, none of the agents—Law, sin, or death—are allowed any access or validity in the realm of the new Christian's walk, which is done in the land of grace-righteousness-life.

There are two historical periods in God's plan of salvation. Before the death of Christ on the cross, and before his resurrection and the coming of the Holy Spirit, the Law was the only restraining force on the planet, to limit the destructiveness of the fallen human heart. That was its sole heaven-sent purpose. A scaffold is necessary to create a building. But it is removed once the building is complete. In the same way, the Law served as a temporary structure to help keep to a minimum the destruction inevitably made by the old heart, and to set the possibility for the future God-provided solution—the new human heart made possible by the resident Holy Spirit. The resurrection of Jesus Christ ushers in a new historical age with the coming of the Holy Spirit, emphatically insisted upon in Rom 8:9–11 as vital to all possibility of understanding the new Christian ethics:

> But you are not in the flesh, you are in the Spirit, if the Spirit of God really dwells in you. Anyone who does not have the Spirit of Christ does not belong to him. But if Christ is in you, although your bodies are dead because of sin, your spirits are alive because of righteousness. If the Spirit of him who raised Jesus from the dead dwells in you, he who raised Christ Jesus from the dead will give life to your mortal bodies also through his Spirit which dwells in you.

Does this mean that the Law is jettisoned completely and ignored by the Christian? Because, this is the main assertion of Pietists, who maintain the necessity of the Law in all ethics, and thereby conclude that all other positions are lawless and anarchic. Of course Christians do not jettison the Law! No Christian has yet graduated from this flesh, which we live in and with, nor has any earthly Christian been yet liberated by what only the resurrection can do—end our fleshly existence. If this is so, then the Law's heaven-sent purpose still obtains—to kill whatever the fleshly power lures us into performing. That such a conflict remains for us to contend with daily, moment by moment, is clearly articulated by Paul in Rom 7:21: "So I find this about *the* law: that when I want to do right, evil lies close at hand" (italics added). (It is critical to notice in verse 23 that Paul's Greek says "*the* law," not as translated in the ESV: "*a* law"—a mere principle. Thus, the entire change in meaning.) A Christian listens to the Law all the time, but with different ears than a non-Christian. The Law, for a Christian, is no longer the ultimate threat, but rather is heard and used as the God-given tool to execute what remains of the old nature. Evidence of this rudimentary fact is recorded in all ancient worship forms that never omit the threefold cry of every Christian: "Christ have mercy, Lord have mercy, Christ have mercy."

Conclusion: "Who will deliver me from this body of death? Thanks be to God through Jesus Christ our Lord! So then, I of myself serve the law of God with my mind, but with my flesh I serve the law of sin" (Rom 7:25). And with this conclusion, the proper foundation has been set to hear about the agent who makes Christian deliverance from this body of death possible—the Holy Spirit. That this deliverance is characterized by continuing mortal combat and conflict within the body is recorded in

8:15ff: "When we cry 'Abba, Father,' it is the Spirit himself bearing witness with our spirit that we are children of God."

Interestingly, for Law-bound Pietists, the evidence for our new walk with God is commonly sought in our triumphs and our victories, such as "Women Aglow." However, Paul comforts believers by asserting that exactly the opposite is true! In Rom 8:15–17, Paul asserts that our assurance does not arrive through human triumphs but rather arrives through the Christian recognition of our abject helplessness—helplessness that God uses to reveal the faithful and unassailable claim of the Holy Spirit that we belong to him. A Christian does not despair over their lack of triumphs, or because he or she increasingly recognizes the enormity of the gulf that lies between what they currently are and what they want to be. Rather, a Christian can find comfort in the fact *that they even recognize* the vast disparity between what they are and what they are called to be. Nonintuitively, it is this very *discomfort* that is the central evidence that they are Jesus's children. A Christian's assurance lies not so much in the triumphs that can also attend this new walk but rather in the Spirit's revelation of the depths of our need. Faith recognizes, with godly confidence, that the suffering of this conflict is not accusatory, but rather is the central evidence that we are being lovingly chosen by God. Faith recognizes, additionally, that the perfection so hoped for has already been granted to us and performed for us, by our incorporation into the body of Christ. Paul says we are righteous *by hope*!

We return now to the issue at hand in 1 Cor 6, where some of the men in the congregation are misusing the freedom of a Christian. Yes, they correctly heard the phrase "All things are lawful." But they take the occasion to abuse this freedom cynically. They seek to justify visiting the red-light district in Corinth by saying "All things are lawful." But Paul emphatically neither backs down on the phrase, which he has preached and which he has emphatically taught, nor does he revert to applying the Law of the old commandment against adultery, which one would expect here. He begins by saying, "All things are lawful, but I will not be enslaved by anything." Later he adds, "All things are lawful, but not all things are helpful. All things are lawful but not all things build up." Instead of using the commandment, he demolishes their cynical action by pointing out their new reality. They are joined to Christ! How could someone joined to Christ take his body that is joined to Christ and join it to a prostitute? There is no excuse for such behavior!

The point here is that Paul's insistence that all things are lawful can still deliver ethically distinct predictable behaviors, *without the Law*, when we by faith recognize that our life is all about Jesus who lives in us. Whoever gratefully rejoices and rightly uses the freedom of the land of grace-righteousness-life will always show in their life specific new behaviors such as mercy and love and joyful service, which are recognized throughout the new community of the body of Christ.

The Case of the Return of Philemon's Runaway Slave

According to the third use of the Law, what should be done with a runaway slave who has robbed his master and repents of his deeds and becomes a Christian? What direction does the third use of the Law give, which, under the Law paradigm of living, requires responses such as "by right," "you must," "you should," "it is necessary," and "this is what is prescribed"? In the if-then land of Law, *if* Onesimus has obviously broken the Law, *then* he must be punished!

Notice, first of all, the complete absence of any of this kind of vocabulary in the entire letter. Instead, we hear the because-therefore vocabulary of freedom and life in the Spirit. The *because* of verses 5–7 is followed by *accordingly* in verse 8. Here, the Law word *command* is ruled out. The contrasting Spirit phrase *I appeal to you* becomes central to the whole letter. Note that Paul does have the authority from his apostolic office within the kingdom of the Spirit to command Philemon, yet, for love's sake, he chooses to appeal. "I, Paul, an ambassador and now a prisoner also for Christ Jesus—I appeal to you for my child, Onesimus" (Phlm 1:9–10). He is talking in the role of a parent in faith to an adult in faith. And, an adult in faith does not use the Law to guide each question regarding the proper ordering of Christian righteousness.

Roman Law prescribes absolute authority of the owner over the slave. Paul has no right to interfere. Paul, Philemon, and Onesimus are all living under Roman Law. How, then, shall Paul, Philemon, and Onesimus live? That is the question. Can Paul fulfill the Law without using the Law? Resoundingly, yes! That is the outcome of this gospel letter.

Paul asserts in Rom 3:31, "Do we overthrow the law by faith? By no means! On the contrary, we uphold the law." Remember that this problem has an intersection with civil Law, the first use of the Law, which is not in contention here. Paul writes concerning a Christian's responsibility under the first use of the Law in Rom 13:1, "Let every person be subject to the governing authorities. For there is no authority except from God, and those that exist have been instituted by God." Paul concedes that "by right" Philemon can avail himself of Roman rules concerning slavery.

So, the question remains: can life be ordered, without using the Law, to guide our behavior? Evidently. Paul is sending Onesimus back without demanding anything from Philemon. But that is not the same as saying Paul does not expect a *specific outcome*. If that is the case, then the Law must not be required to produce specific outcomes. Love, produced by the Holy Spirit, can and will produce specific outcomes.

Is the Law required to maintain right interpersonal relationships? Evidently not. "I preferred to do nothing without your consent, in order that your goodness might be not by compulsion, but of your own free will" (v. 14). "So, if you consider me your partner, receive him as you would receive me" (v. 17).

The result: "Confident of your obedience, I write to you, knowing that you will do even more than I say" (v. 21). Here, good Pietists would leap up and shout, "Do you not see that word *obedience*? That is a Law word!" No, that obedience arises not from an if-then word of Law, but rather arises from a because-therefore word of freedom:

- "Because I hear of your love, and of the faith that you have toward the Lord Jesus" (v. 5),
- because "I have derived much joy and comfort from your love" (v. 7),
- because "I preferred to do nothing without your consent, in order that your goodness might not be by *compulsion* but of your own accord" (v. 14; italics added),
- because you can have him back "no longer as a slave, but more than a slave, as a beloved brother" (v. 16), and
- because Onesimus is now my brother in the Lord and your brother, too (v. 16).

Therefore, "confident of your obedience . . ." (v. 21).

Specific outcome: So, evidently Onesimus will not be subjected by Philemon to capital punishment on his return, but, rather, transformed by Christ, will return to his old responsibilities with a new, free relationship to his old owner, now become his boss. Will he now have a salary for his work? We don't know. But I am sure that would be part of Philemon's "doing more than Paul asks."

- Are the Law's requirements to love your neighbor as yourself fulfilled here? Yes.
- Are the Law's requirements to show mercy fulfilled here? Yes.
- Are the Law's requirements to love God fulfilled here? Yes.
- Are the Law's demands that our lives be transformed fulfilled here? Yes.
- Was the third use of the Law required to produce any of these outcomes. No.
- Does the Law demand transformation of our lives? Yes.
- But can the Law produce such transformation, let alone anything resembling this kind of result? No.
- Does God alone, with the working of the indwelling Holy Spirit, provide the power to transform our lives? Yes.
- Is transformation under the wonderful freedom provided by the Spirit's guidance the point of what is depicted here in this gospel story? Yes!

In summary, third-use thinking is here utterly demolished by this real-life demonstration of the absolute contrast between walking by the Spirit and walking by the Law. These two alternatives constitute an absolute either-or. To try to assimilate the two into a companionship, or into an amalgamation, is not only impossible, but any such effort will only guarantee that one will lose Christ in the bargain. "For freedom Christ has set us fee. Stand fast, therefore, and do not submit again to a yoke of slavery!" (Gal 5:1).

Away, then, with all this mumbling about the necessity of the Law being a Christian's guide.

The Case of the Potluck in Antioch

In the world of commerce, the rule is "follow the money." In the world of the church, the rule is "follow the recognized authority." We saw this rule played out in the Reformation collision between two contending authorities, and we see it at this potluck. For this is nothing less than a frontal collision between the two primary authorities of the new church. The first authority is the initial leadership of the faith, represented by James, in Jerusalem. The other authority is the arrival of the new gospel-to-the-gentiles leadership authority of Paul, authored by what Jesus revealed to him. The content of what that authority revealed is most clearly laid out in Paul's preaching for the rest of the book of Galatians.

James, the brother of Jesus, presides at Jerusalem and even seems to supersede Peter as the old guard. Like Melanchthon, who betrayed his best friend Luther's central rediscovery of God in the Reformation (only after Luther died), James appears reluctant to accede completely to the new freedom completed by Jesus's imputed righteousness. Implicitly he still straddles the fence, like all Pietists, in demanding *some* structure from the Law. He seems to find that Jesus's breathtaking statement that "all foods are now kosher" too extreme (Mark 7:19). Surely the old covenant, including most of the book of Leviticus, cannot be thus completely jettisoned! Surely it must still obtain in securing some structure to the new life of freedom in Christ.

What happens at this potluck is of little *apparent* significance. When James's Jerusalem authorities come through the door, Peter just quietly moves from the gentile table over to the Jewish table. Apparently, Peter is afraid that he will be seen by these authorities as disrespecting the Law regarding kosher conduct. Critical for non-Jewish readers to understand is that kosher laws are vital and central to the faith of Judaism. Although in Hebrew *kosher* technically means "fit" or "proper," especially with regard to what is eaten, the concept of kosher in Judaism is closely tied to the idea of being "unclean." According to the Torah, only certain animals are considered "clean" for consumption, and the laws of Lev 11:47 distinguish between creatures that may be eaten and those that may not. This dietary law is part of a broader set of laws that also address ritual purity and the separation of the Israelites from other nations. The Torah's dietary laws are not just about food but also about the moral and spiritual implications. Although such cleanness is not quite salvific, it is critically central to righteousness. *Kosher* provides a whole mental map for an observant Jew to navigate a world where so much defiles. As with every Law, it demands. Just imagine the conceptual nuclear explosion that results, ethically, when Jesus abrogates these demands! In Mark 7:19, Jesus declared all foods clean; and again Jesus says in John 15:3, "Already you are clean because of the word that I have spoken to you." So, Peter is also straddling the fence, seeming to acknowledge that the Law's continuing function is necessary to direct clean behavior. He thus compromises the freedom every Christian has in Christ.

Either Christ makes us clean or we make ourselves clean. Jesus said, "Already you are clean because of the word that I have spoken to you" (John 15:3). There is no compromise. Faith in one alternative completely demolishes the other. Each faith is completely antagonistic to the other. Only one can obtain. Only one truth can be still standing after the conflict. This truth of the gospel is what Paul instantly stands up to defend. Imagine that moment! The two monumental leaders of the new faith are in very public contention, leading to the humiliation of at least Peter, if not the whole Jerusalem faction.

Cleanness aside, and more vital still, we see that wherever the Law is held to obtain, *there is no freedom*. Paul writes with a repeated characteristic throughout his letters—he titles each major section of his writing with a summary statement. Examples of this are Rom 1:16–17, 12:1–2, and 1 Cor 1:18. Paul arrives at his climactic statement in the whole book of Galatians in chapter 5, verse 1, where he proclaims in summary, "For freedom Christ has set us free. Stand fast therefore and do not submit again to a yoke of slavery." Later in the paragraph he writes, "For you were called to freedom brethren; only do not use your freedom as an opportunity for the flesh, but through love be servants of one another. For the whole law is fulfilled in one word, 'you shall love your neighbor as yourself'" (vv. 13–14).

It takes a good soldier of Christ, not only to recognize that Peter's apparently simple movement from one table to another betrayed the whole gospel of Jesus Christ, but to unhesitatingly, staunchly, and against all rules of human decorum publicly call it out for what it was, and to declare the truth of the gospel in opposition to such bondage to the old Law.

In summary, these five cases, with their various facets, reveal that the freedom that Christians have been given through the completed and imputed righteousness of Jesus allows us to pursue our lives without the necessity of being hounded, driven, or terrified by the Law. Instead, we "present [ourselves] to God as those who have been brought from death to life, and [our] members to God as instruments for righteousness" (Rom 6:13). We perform whatever service God has equipped us to do, through each of the various endowed personal charismata, so that wherever and whenever our work is done in faith, it pleases him.

CHAPTER 8

Luther's Vocabulary Regarding the Law

ENGAGING WITH WHAT LUTHER wrote is to embark upon an entire sea of manuscripts, including, but not limited to: commentaries on scriptural books, treatises, letters, disputations, table talks, and about twenty-three hundred sermons existing from the seven thousand that he preached. The task here cannot be to peruse the entire contents of these manuscripts to discover in them everything Luther wrote concerning the Law. Rather, it is just as effective to demonstrate from a few critical sources how consistent Luther was in his understanding of the Law, which he always passionately expressed and never departed from. To make the case that Luther understood only two uses of the Law, it will suffice to use only the (later) 1531 Galatians commentary and the *Antinomian Disputations* from 1538. These serve as two demonstrations of the most mature and definitive expressions of Luther's theology. To additionally buttress the case against Pietism and its imagined third use of the Law, one can also adduce Luther's ministry-long repeated concepts such as:

- *Simul justus et peccator:* Luther's unique formulation that expresses the Pauline concept that a Christian is 100 percent righteous and 100 percent sinner, *at the same time.*
- *Lex semper accusat:* Luther insists, everywhere and always, that the Law *always* and only accuses and is never anyone's friend, even if one is a Christian.
- *Conscience:* The venue that receives the word as a personal address from God.
- *The five solas:* Each one of these prevents any theological notion of a cooperative concept of salvation, either in justification or in sanctification.

One last preliminary concept needs to be clearly understood. Luther never treated the Law as an abstraction. He always treated all of God's word, not as something that operated at the level of signification or symbol, but rather as a power that engaged a person at the level of *effect*. God's word *happens*. It always does what it says. It comes as an *event*. Genesis 1:3, 6, 7, 9, 11, 14, 20, 24, 26; Isa 55:10–11; and Jesus calming the storm and raising Lazarus from the dead serve as just a few examples. Whenever Jesus preaches division happens. Without fail, some believe, some actively disbelieve. Consider, also, what happens when any prophet begins with the awesome preface "Thus says the Lord!" Such proclamation always caused something to happen or predicted that it would happen. If so, God's word, whether read or heard, always arrives as event, by doing something to you. Although this way of treating Scripture is implicit, and not explicitly stated by Luther, it is evident in Luther's refusal to deal with theology by writing a dogmatic systematics, but rather by asserting that the only valid function theology has is to lead to proclamation. He insisted that every other use of theology was pure poison! For him, proclamation is always event. Thus, the church becomes a "mouth house."

So, in the case of the Law, Luther never treats it as a magnificent abstraction. He adamantly refuses to discuss the Law in any other way than by locating what it does. He insists that any valid discussion of the Law can be located only by the description of its action. That is, any discussion of the Law has to deal solely with what the Law always accomplishes at the level of effect. The central error made by Melanchthon is to treat the Law as a philosophical abstraction that can be dealt with merely at the level of signification. He is the one who insists upon systematization of theology, thus making it into an abstraction. Melanchthon posits an imaginary concept called *lex aeterna* (the eternal Law), which imagines a way in which the Law can be benign and not accusatory. This concept serves as the main critical theological foundation to create any possibility for a third use of the Law. This has been dealt with more fully previously.

In contrast to that, what Luther observed in Scripture is that proclamation is never a lecture "about something" but rather a confrontation that does something to the hearer. In the case of the Law, it always terrifies. It always kills. The preaching of Amos shows how this is done: "Because I will do this to you, prepare to meet your God, O Israel!" (Amos 4:12). Here the Law is neither informational nor benign, but rightly and properly confrontational. The Law is thunder and storm! John the Baptist did not draw out crowds from Jerusalem by being informational, but by preaching thunder, confronting people with their helplessness in their sin, and by fearlessly exposing the priests and faculty at Jerusalem for their lack of such proclamation. Jesus's preaching in the Sermon on the Mount wields the Law confrontationally: "Unless your righteousness far exceeds that of the scribes and the Pharisees, you will never[, ever] enter the kingdom of heaven" (Matt 5:20). Jesus here decidedly rejects all use of the Law as a benign to-do list. Paul summarizes the argument of chapters two and three of Romans with the following proclamation:

> Now we know that whatever the law says it speaks to those who are under the law so that every mouth may be stopped, and the whole world may be held accountable to God. For no human being will be justified in his sight by works of the law, since through the law comes the knowledge of sin. (Rom 3:19–20)

In the First Great Awaking of the American colonies, Jonathan Edwards preached fiery sermons up and down the East Coast, such as the one titled "Sinners in the Hand of an Angry God." These sermons caused his hearers to cry out in anguish. These sermons of the First Great Awakening changed the history of the United States, arguably uniting the colonies against the tyranny of being treated as subjects rather than fellow citizens of England.

Everywhere in Scripture Luther found that the Law always accuses. The primary feature that distinguishes a sermon from a lecture is that a biblical preacher knows that proclamation is not a lecture! A true proclaimer deals with dynamite and trusts God to do whatever is needed, provided that he or she sticks to what they are authorized by that word to say.

Luther refuses to misuse the Law in proclamation by understanding it as something benign so that it can serve as a directing lecture "about something" for the newly able Christian to perform. That is to make two egregious errors. First, such a "sermon" becomes very much like reading an instructional manual for assembling a piece of Ikea furniture and ends up being just about as exciting. No wonder so much snoozing occurs. No wonder impatient hearers look at their watch to see when such a lecture will finally end. Nor does it help to pass out notes with blanks to be filled in during such a "sermon." Second, and more damning, is that the subject agent in such lectures becomes you, you, you, rather than hearing much about Jesus. For instance, "Here is how you, too, can become a Christian athlete, or how you, too, can control bad emotions, or (best of all) how you can rejoice constantly." Such lectures, passed off as proclamation, live in an entirely different universe than the proclamation of the Law found in the Old Testament, in Jesus, in the Gospels, or in the Epistles.

The 1531 Galatians Commentary

Luther's entire preface to this commentary deals with proper proclamation so that the hearer can finally arrive at proper Christian assurance. To anchor both of these, Luther insists that the hearer understands the concept *passive righteousness*. That becomes the thematic foundation, not only for the introduction, but for the entire commentary.

"Luther's *Lectures on Galatians* of 1531 deserves to be called a declaration of Christian independence—of independence from the Law and from anything or anyone else except the God and Father of our Lord Jesus Christ."[1]

To secure that freedom, Luther's term *passive righteousness* expresses the obvious fact that such righteousness cannot be active—that is, by any human effort or will—but must be a righteousness created and given by Christ's action alone. Christ's righteousness and human righteousness cannot be combined as Paul points out in Phil 3, but are absolutely antithetical to each other, and even annihilate each other! So, Luther's term *passive righteousness* denotes Christ's righteousness. It absolutely excludes any concept of renewed human righteousness coordinating with Christ's righteousness (our new standing in justification) to now be newly able to keep the Law (Pietism). By *passive* Luther means exactly that, in the strictest sense. Humans have absolutely nothing to do with either the righteousness that comes with being justified, or with any subsequent improvement that comes by the work of the indwelling Spirit in sanctification. Any introduction of the latter instantly removes all assurance, and with it all Christian freedom. With this imagined coordination, once again, humans are trapped and enslaved by the question, "When have you done enough?" There is no end to the requirements of the Law! "Do you not hear the law?" (Gal 4:21). Luther writes, "We have taken it upon ourselves in the Lord's name to lecture on this Epistle of Paul to the Galatians . . . [because] there is a clear and present danger that the devil may take away from us the pure doctrine of faith and may substitute for it the doctrines of works."[2]

---

1. Pelikan, *LW* 26:ix.
2. *LW* 26:3.

Luther lists the various kinds of righteousness—political, ceremonial, the righteousness of the Decalogue, and the righteousness of faith. The righteousness of faith has carefully to be distinguished from the others.

> This most excellent righteousness, the righteousness of faith, which God imputes to us through Christ without works, is neither political, nor ceremonial, nor legal, nor work-righteousness, but is quite the opposite; it is a merely passive righteousness, while all the other, listed above, are active. For here we work nothing, render nothing to God; we only receive and permit someone else to work in us, namely God. Therefore, it is appropriate to call the righteousness of faith or Christian righteousness "passive." This is a righteousness hidden in a mystery which the world does not understand. In fact, Christians themselves do not adequately understand it or grasp it in the midst of their temptations. Therefore, it must always be taught and continually exercised. And anyone who does not grasp or take hold of it in affliction and terrors of conscience cannot stand. For there is no comfort of conscience so solid and certain as is this passive righteousness.[3]

> This passive righteousness says with confidence: "I do not seek active righteousness. I ought to have and perform it; but I declare that even if I did have it and perform it, I cannot trust in it or stand up before the judgment of God on the basis of it. Thus I put myself beyond all active righteousness, all righteousness of my own, or of the divine Law, and I embrace only that passive righteousness which is the righteousness of grace, mercy, and the forgiveness of sins."[4]

Luther continues his argument by referring to the two Pauline kingdoms that are the foundation for Paul's new ethical teaching. These mortally opposed kingdoms are composed of component parts that absolutely destroy and annihilate the other. The three parts of each kingdom are inextricably united. To review, the three parts of each kingdom are also exact correlates of their adversarial component powers. The kingdom of grace-righteousness-life is sent to annihilate each member of Law-sin-death (Rom 5:20–21). Grace annihilates Law. Righteousness annihilates sin. Life annihilates death. By baptism we are joined to the death of Christ so that the Law can no longer get any work out of a dead slave.

3. *LW* 26:4–5.
4. *LW* 26:6.

The new man[5] in Christ is set free from the Law because beyond death, the Law cannot reach him. And a whole new world of Law-free ethics is introduced. Thus, the dying is critical. This is what Pietism does not understand. Pietism tries to improve the deathless old man. In contrast, faith trusts the imputed righteousness of Christ that uniquely defines the once buried, and now resurrected new person.

Luther writes that it would be a bad dialectician who does not properly distinguish between these two righteousnesses—the active and the passive. "But when I go beyond the old man, I also go beyond the Law. For the flesh or the old man, the Law and works are all joined together. In the same way the Spirit or the new man is joined to the promise and to grace."[6]

Now Luther continues with the assertions that drive Pietists crazy.

> Sin cannot happen in this Christian righteousness; for where there is no Law, there cannot be any transgression (Rom. 4:15). If, therefore, sin does not have a place here, there is no conscience, no terror, no sadness. Therefore, John says: "No one born of God commits sin" (1 John 3:9). But if there is any conscience or fear present, this is a sign that this righteousness has been withdrawn that grace has been lost sight of, and that Christ is hidden and out of sight.[7]

Luther continues his argument to build upon the only foundation where Christian assurance is possible—that is, by Christ's creation of a new passive righteousness. A unique characteristic required to produce the new assurance is the amazing fact that a Christian becomes 100 percent righteous and 100 percent sinner, at the same time.

> I am indeed a sinner according to the present life and its righteousness, as a son of Adam, where the Law accuses me, death reigns and devours me. But above this life I have another righteousness, another life, which is Christ, the Son of God, who does not know sin and death, but is righteousness and eternal life. For His sake this body of mine will be raised from the dead and delivered from the slavery of the Law and sin and will be sanctified together with the spirit. *Thus, as we live here, both remain.*[8]

---

5. Here and in what follows, the term *man* will be used instead of the more cumbersome equivalents to refer to all humanity.

6. *LW* 26:7.

7. *LW* 26:8.

8. *LW* 26:9; italics added.

All proclamation should be clearly characterized by these two assertions. It becomes the hallmark of true Reformation preaching. Without a clear proclamation of passive righteousness, all is lost.

> Therefore I admonish you, especially those of you who are to become instructors of consciences, as well as each of you individually, that you exercise yourselves by study, by reading, by meditation, and by prayer, so that in temptation you will be able to instruct consciences, both you own and others, console them, and take them from the Law to grace, from active righteousness to passive righteousness, in short, from Moses to Christ.[9]

Such preaching is critical in a Christian's struggle of faith and for faith, because,

> When it comes to experience, you will find the Gospel a rare guest but the Law a constant guest in your conscience, which is habituated to the Law and the sense of sin; reason, too, supports this sense.[10]

He previously said,

> So far as the words are concerned, we know all this very well and can discourse on it. But in the struggle, when the devils try to mar the image of Christ and to snatch the Word from our hearts, we discover that we do not know them as well as we should. Whoever could define Christ accurately then, exalting Him and looking to Him as his sweet Savior and High Priest and not as a stern Judge, would have overcome all evils and would already be in the kingdom of heaven. But to do this in the midst of struggle is the hardest thing there is.[11]

Luther takes Paul's preaching about the two opposing kingdoms of Law-sin-death and grace-righteousness-life and helpfully lays out the right use of the Law. This happens only when the Law stays in its proper and restricted lane.

> The Law must not exceed its limits but should have its dominion only over the flesh, which is subjected to it and remains under it. When this is the case, the Law remains within its limits. But if it wants to ascend into the conscience and exert its rule there, see to it that you are a good dialectician and that you make the

---

9. *LW* 26:10.
10. *LW* 26:117.
11. *LW* 26:38.

correct distinction. Give no more to the Law than it has coming, and say to it . . . "Stay within your limits, and exercise your dominion over the flesh. You shall not touch my conscience. For I am baptized; and through the Gospel I have been called to a fellowship of righteousness and eternal life, to the kingdom of Christ in which my conscience is at peace, where there is no Law, but only the forgiveness of sins, peace, quiet, happiness, salvation, and eternal life."[12]

The following lengthy citations from Luther's Galatians commentary can stand alone in making and defending his point regarding the Law's limitations. Luther leaves absolutely no room here for an imagined third use of the Law.

As I often insist, therefore, these two, the Law and the promise must be very carefully distinguished for they are as far apart in time, place, person, and all features as heaven and earth. They should be separated as far as possible, in such a way that the Law has dominion over the flesh, but the promise reigns sweetly in the conscience. They are indeed close together, because they are joined in one man or in one soul. If you assign a specific place to each one this way, you walk safely between them.[13]

Paul urged this argument so diligently; for he saw that in the church this evil would arise, namely, that the Word of God would be confused, which means that the Promise would be mixed with the Law and in this way be completely lost. For when the promise is mixed up with the Law, it becomes Law pure and simple. . . . Accustom yourself to distinguish the Law from the promise even in time, so that when the Law comes and accuses your conscience, you say, "Lady Law, you are not coming on time; you are too late. I am living after the revelation of Christ, who has abrogated and abolished you."[14]

"If the Law does not justify, why, then, was it given?" Again: "Why does God prod and burden us with the Law if it does not give life?" Therefore, this is a difficult question. Reason is brought short by it and cannot answer it but is offended by it in the highest degree. Because reason does not know anything except the Law, it necessarily deals with this and supposes that

---

12. *LW* 26:11.
13. *LW* 26:301.
14. *LW* 26:302; italics added.

righteousness is attained through it. . . . For when the rabble hear from the Gospel that righteousness comes by the sheer grace of God and by faith alone, without the Law or works, they draw the same conclusion the Jews drew then: "Then let us not do any work!"[15]

Here one must know that there is a *double use of the Law*. One is the civic use. . . . Thus the first understanding and use of the Law is restrain the wicked. . . . The other use of the Law is the theological or spiritual one, *which serves to increase transgressions*. This is the primary purpose of the Law of Moses, that through it sin might grow and be multiplied. . . . Therefore the true function and chief and proper use of the Law is to reveal to man his sin, blindness, misery, wickedness, ignorance, hate and contempt of God. . . . To curb and crush this monster and raging beast, that is *the presumption of religion*, God is obliged, on Mt. Sinai, to give a new Law with such an awesome spectacle that the entire people is crushed with fear. . . . *Therefore, the Law is intent only on this beast not on any other.*[16]

I urge you, who are to be the teachers of other, to learn this doctrine of the true and proper use of the Law carefully; for after our time it will be obscured again and will be completely wiped out. . . . Therefore it is a matter of no small moment to believe correctly about what the Law is, and what its use and function are. Thus, it is evident that we do not reject the Law and works, as our opponents falsely accuse us. But we do everything to establish the Law and we require works. We say that the Law is good and useful, but in its proper use, namely *first* as we have said earlier, to restrain civic transgression, and *secondly* to reveal spiritual transgression. Therefore, the Law is a light that illumines and shows, not the grace of God or righteousness and life, but the wrath of God, sin, death, our damnation in the sight of God, and hell.[17]

The foolishness of the human heart is so great that in its conflict of conscience, when the Law performs its function and carries out its true use, the heart not only doesn't take hold of the doctrine of grace, which gives a sure promise of the forgiveness of sins for the sake of Christ but *it actually looks for more laws to*

---

15. *LW* 26:304–5.
16. *LW* 26:308–9; italics added.
17. *LW* 26:312; italics added.

help it out. "If I live longer," it says, "I shall improve my life. I shall do that and that. I shall enter a monastery, I shall live frugally and content myself with bread and water, I shall go about barefoot. . . . *Unless you do the very opposite here,* that is, unless you send Moses and his Law away to the smug and stubborn, and unless you, in your fears and terrors, take hold of Christ who suffered and was crucified, and died for your sins, *your salvation is over and done with.* . . . Therefore, if you have been crushed by that hammer, do not use your contrition wrongly by burdening yourself with even more laws. Listen to Christ when He says (Matt. 11:28): "Come to me, all who labor and are heavy laden, and I will give you rest."[18]

In Christian theology and according to its proper description, the Law does not justify but has exactly the opposite effect: it discloses us to ourselves; it shows us a wrathful God; it manifests wrath; it terrifies us.[19]

Before the Law comes, I am smug and do not worry about sin; when the Law comes it shows me sin, death, and hell. Surely this is not being justified, it is being sentenced, being made an enemy of God being condemned to death and hell. Therefore, the principal purpose of the Law in theology is to make men not better but worse; that is, it shows them their sin, so that by the recognition of sin they may be humbled, frightened and worn down, and so may long for grace and for the Blessed Offspring. This is a summary of the argument of Paul.[20]

Therefore the function of the Law is only to kill, yet in such a way that God may be able to make alive . . . *in order that this beast, the presumption of righteousness, may be killed, since man cannot live unless it is killed.*[21]

In summary:

- These selected few citations should be enough to show that, in Luther, the Law is never a Christian's friend, nor anyone's friend.

---

18. *LW* 26:315–16; italics added.
19. *LW* 26:326.
20. *LW* 26:327.
21. *LW* 26:335; italics added.

- The proper theological function of the Law is not to make men better, but to make them worse.
- That, for Luther, unless you do the opposite of looking for more laws to help out, "Your salvation is over."
- When the Law is mixed with promise, it becomes Law, pure and simple.
- Together, all the above make the third use of the Law not only impossible but lethal to any hope of assurance.

If we call ourselves followers of the Reformation, this is what we insist upon. More importantly, if we call ourselves Christians who follow Paul, this is what we insist upon and confess, gladly and in spite of the horrible opposition that always arises against this teaching.

Conscience and the Law in Luther

Since the concept of conscience is so vital, not only in the citations above, but everywhere in Luther's writings, it is necessary to establish a working definition that avoids the hopelessly misleading pseudo-psychological concepts that currently carry the same name. The simplest definition is that for Luther, the conscience constitutes the venue "Where God Meets Man." This is the location where the mortal battle is fought for assurance, where the accusing voice of the Law is heard, always alternating with the voice of the promise. It is in the conscience where the battle is fought over which of these two mortally opposing powers will have the final authoritative say. Will it be the Law? Or will it be the word of promise, the Gift of Jesus's indwelling Spirit?

> Why did [Luther] take up the pen? The primary reason was not the urge of the scholar nor the controversial zeal of a reformer, but the responsibility of a pastor for a pure, clear, comprehensible, convincing and liberating proclamation of the gospel. He had himself struggled to understand the righteousness of God, which, as the gospel reveals means that the righteous live by faith.[22]

> There followed a succession of German devotional works . . . exclusively concerned with what makes a man a Christian: expositions of the Ten Commandments or the Lord's Prayer . . . and,

---

22. Ebeling, *Luther*, 55.

the crown of this whole literature, the "Treatise on Good Works" and the treatise "On the Freedom of a Christian."[23]

These are the words of one who spoke to his own time what it needed to hear, words uttered with the compelling force of what can be uttered in the light of the day, with the liberty of one who is completely absorbed by what he has to say, and with the practicality of one who is hitting the nail right on the head. His word is drawn from the holy scripture and inspired by it alone. . . . *The holy scriptures and the present day intersect as it were at a single point, in the conscience that hears the word.* It was Luther's concern that the word of God should be heard in this way.[24]

But if Christ is the fundamental meaning, so that in him all words form a single word, then their application to the individual . . . must consist not of disconnected useful moral applications, nor of a demand for similar works on the part of man, *but must be aimed solely at the faith which apprehends Christ.* . . . We may say also that we find here an understanding of the Holy Spirit strictly orientated towards the crucified Christ.[25]

Christian preaching is the process in which the distinction between the law and the gospel takes place. . . . The concern of Christian preaching is to put into practice the distinction between the law and the gospel, that is, to carry on the progress of a battle, in which time and again the distinction between the law and the gospel is newly at issue and is made in practice. . . . But if the process of preaching is what it claims to be, that is, the process of salvation, then as the distinction is made between the law and the gospel, so the event of salvation takes place. And a confusion of the two is not a misfortune of little significance, a regrettable weakness, but is evil in the strict sense, the total opposite of salvation.[26]

Every person's conscience acts with authority. In fact, a non-Christian conscience asserts its decrees as absolute, final, and not subject to any appeal. However, it does so in its failure to recognize that every conscience that is without the deliverance of an alien righteousness is

---

23. Ebeling, *Luther*, 55.
24. Ebeling, *Luther*, 58; italics added.
25. Ebeling, *Luther*, 105; italics added.
26. Ebeling, *Luther*, 117.

helplessly subject to another *higher* authority than itself—the Law. Since, as Luther rightly and consistently points out, the Law always accuses, the result is inevitable—a bad conscience. Without Christ, *bad* and *conscience* are synonymous, forming a tautology. The bondage of this combination is the birthplace of regret, anguish, despair, low self-esteem, and the need to project and blame our failures on others.

Luther, from his experience of anguish under this accusing Law, correctly identified this place, called conscience, as the location where Christ's rescue from the Law takes place. In *The Bondage of the Will* Luther writes,

> The prince of this world's purpose is to capture and bind consciences. This, the true God cannot tolerate, and so the Word of God and the traditions of men are irreconcilably opposed to one another, precisely as God himself and Satan are mutually opposed, each destroying the works and subverting the dogmas of the other like two kings laying waste each other's kingdoms.[27]

The problem is that such a rescue of the conscience requires an even higher authority than either conscience or Law. Luther claimed his own deliverance from Paul's word in Rom 6. He found there that since the Law's accusation never ceases regarding our existence in the flesh, its former slave must die in order to be delivered from that accusing voice. In his Romans commentary Luther called this deliverance through being baptized into Christ's death, not the exodus from *vice* to *virtue*, but the exodus from *virtue* to *grace*. This deliverance of his conscience arrived only through passive righteousness—the complete righteousness that belongs to Christ, but which is counted to us by faith. This deliverance comes by hearing and is effected by continuing to hear the dynamic word of promise. Since the death of the Law's old slave happened when we were joined to Christ's death in baptism, Luther had a final defense under every renewed attack of the Law's accusation. He would stoutly say, "God does not lie!" For him this was synonymous with saying, "I am baptized!" With this scriptural word he insisted that he was dead to his former accuser. In this way he used the promise of Christ's alien righteousness to end the voice of the Law.

As a compassionate pastor, Luther recognized that this precise conflict takes place in every Christian. Since such deliverance comes only through hearing the word of promise, the whole Reformation project

---

27. *LW* 33:54.

became the need to restore right proclamation. So it became his duty to proclaim not only where he had found deliverance, but to identify for all of us that our death in baptism, together with Christ's righteousness being counted to us, formed our only possible deliverance from an accusing conscience. That deliverance creates a unique creation of God—one who is 100 percent sinner and yet 100 percent righteous *at the same time* (*simul justus et peccator*).

The established conscience along with the nonintuitive knowledge that we are 100 percent righteous while at the same time being constantly accused together form the only possible foundation on this earth for proper Christian assurance. This assurance is at work in us both in the present and most importantly at our last moment.

Two scriptures are important to cite regarding this point. The apostle Peter writes, "In the days of Noah . . . eight persons were brought safely through water." (This is passive.) "Baptism, which corresponds to this, now saves you, not as a removal of dirt from the body but as an appeal to God for a good conscience, through the resurrection of Jesus Christ . . . with all powers having been subjected to him" (1 Pet 3:20-22). The apostle John adds, "Whenever our hearts condemn us, God is greater than our heart, and he knows everything. Beloved, if our heart does not condemn us, we have confidence before God" (1 John 3:20-21).

Luther insisted, especially in the Galatians commentary, that the object for all preaching was to "establish the conscience," firm in the assurance that could only come from a perfect righteousness. It formed the basis of his entire sea of letters, treatises, and sermons. But this assurance arises only from a continuing, incessant, and unending mortal conflict in the conscience over which voice it is currently hearing. Hearing only the word of promise as the final authority, the last word, over the accused conscience is the final defense that only a Christian can assert in this struggle. It is an art, says Luther, which he, as a longtime doctor of theology, has never yet fully mastered.

In order for Reformed proclamation to establish the conscience secure in a complete yet alien righteousness, every false anthropological assumption that mankind had a free will had to be extinguished. This was the entire thesis of Luther's magnum opus and longest treatise, *The Bondage of the Will* (or, more accurately, *The Captivation of the Will*). The assertion of a free will understood narrowly *with regard to its imagined ability to cooperate in our salvation* is deadly to any hope of an established conscience, for the simple reason that no one can assert with finality that one has ever fully completed the moral requirements of that task. And so, the two mathematical and annihilating alternatives presented by Luther in this work are:

(a) a free will, but then the inevitably resulting "bound conscience," or,

(b) a bound will, but then an "established conscience," where God does everything (the *sola*, God alone).

> The words of the Law are spoken, therefore, not to affirm the power of the will, but to enlighten blind reason and make it see that its own light is no light and that the virtue of the will is no virtue. "Through the Law," says Paul, "comes the knowledge of sin" (Rom. 3:20); ... the whole meaning and purpose of the Law is simply to furnish knowledge, and that of nothing but sin; it is *not* to reveal or confer any *power*. For this knowledge is not power, nor does it confer power, but it instructs and shows that there is no power there, and how great a *weakness* there is.[28]

> Accordingly, it is Satan's work to prevent men from recognizing their plight and to keep them presuming that they can do everything they are told. But the work of Moses or a lawgiver is the opposite of this, namely, to make man's plight plain to him by means of the Law and thus to break and confound him by self-knowledge, so as to prepare him for grace and send him to Christ that he may be saved.[29]

If the forgoing point is true, then it has profound inescapable ramifications for proclamation. No longer is the preacher a prosecuting lawyer for God seeking to bring in a positive verdict from you, the jury. (Where the preacher must, by extension, rely upon rhetorical powers to win the day, and necessarily to "dress up" God to make him attractive to the hearers.) Instead, the preacher now arrives with a word that is correctly heard as the feared executioner of every false human hope that salvation ever had any relation to a do-it-yourself project. That is, he rightly preaches the Law's killing function, killing the beast of the false hope of human righteousness. This is its only God-given function. Only then do hearers cry out for the promise, the sheer gift, the righteousness that belongs to Jesus, but is now, with great joy and assurance, proclaimed as counted to them.

---

28. *LW* 33:127; italics added.
29. *LW* 33:130.

Because we remain in the flesh, God's loving and faithful word of deliverance always has to arrive first as accusation. As Luther would charmingly say, "God has first to be your devil before He can be your savior." The unique Reformation concept is that man and God are not related by analogy, as the scholastics taught, but rather by contradiction. This also enters into any discussion of Luther's concept of conscience. This nonintuitive form of salvation arises because God meets us in the conscience by *confrontation*.

> The Word of God is not taken seriously as such if it does not become, not merely as the Law but in the proper sense as the Gospel, *our "opponent,"* that is, the Word which effects in us the opposite of what we are. 1) As the Word of the Creator it creates from nothing. 2) As the Word of Law it destroys our own righteousness and self-assertion in the sight of God. 3) As the Word of the Gospel it declares the sinner righteous. "When the Word of God comes, it runs contrary to our thought and desire."[30]

> True Faith has to do with being confronted with Another who makes us relinquish our own calculations and thoughts, wishes and hopes, and who breaks into our lives as a foreign reality, insisting that we recognize Him as such. . . . The judgment of God over people and their being, their will and their inner life is diametrically opposed to what people want to believe about themselves. Thus, *wherever God's Word meets us, it meets us as the enemy*. For wherever God's Word is portrayed so as to be in accord with people's hopes and desires and wherever it is accepted as a truth that corresponds with their preconceptions, then we know right away that it is not God's Word we are dealing with. . . . In this sense, all religion—inasmuch as it transmits human will and striving into an idea of God—is an especially sophisticated and spiritual form of *annihilating God*. In such a transfer, however, God is not justified in men, but men are justified in God.[31]

> The problem arises because we are trapped in bondage and so cannot, will not, desist from seeking to manipulate God according to our own projects. God is indeed love, but we will not have it. Nothing is more threatening than a love or mercy that takes over the destiny of those who want to be gods. The declaration

---

30. *WA* 56:423n19; italics added.
31. Iwand, *Righteousness of Faith*, 22; italics added.

of love—"I will have mercy on whom I will have mercy"—taken in the abstract is the most threatening of all, because we do not know upon whom, in particular, God desires to have mercy. Everything turns to wrath and such wrath never ends in this age. God, as we have said repeatedly, simply cannot actually have mercy in the abstract. For God actually to have mercy God must die as abstraction and we must die as would-be gods. So, Jesus' death engenders the Word that ends the abstraction, the wrath of God, and ends our lives as would-be gods at once. Jesus dies for us and so in the end of the God of wrath and the beginning of actual love when he is proclaimed and received in Faith. . . . Wrath always threatens. But we are baptized and the Word has broken in upon us. We shall need to hear it again and again.[32]

Luther places an either/or here, too. In every transformation something constant must be in place so that the transformation is possible. If a person is to change, then God must remain constant. In this way, faith in the faithfulness of God is in his Word, or, as Luther liked to say, the basis for the transformation of man is in the truthfulness and steadfastness of God, namely in His Word. If, however a person will not be changed and will rather remain what he or she already is, that person will try to change God's Word and will try to redefine it in human terms—both in its interpretation and in its teaching. . . . Either God is constant in His Word and we are the ones who are changed, or man is true to himself and for him God's Word becomes a relative, human enterprise of religious opinions and ideas.[33]

This is how the conscience becomes an established conscience, miraculously, through the Holy Spirit's imprinting upon us the word of promise as sheer gift to us. Christians no longer suffer the anguish or the hell of a "bad" conscience. The established conscience is the definition of salvation according to Luther. Everything happens in that venue.

Luther and the Antinomian Dispute

The antinomian dispute is no arcane philosophical dispute to be dealt with only by scholars of theology. It deals with a vitally important

---

32. Forde, *Theology Is for Proclamation*, 131.
33. Iwand, *Righteousness of Faith*, 22

question asked by every thoughtful Christian: "Does the Law have any continuing function in my new Christian behavior?"

Anti (Greek meaning "against") *nomos* (Greek, meaning "law").[34] Thus, antinomianism is any view that rejects the Law or any system of Law as regulatory for human behavior. This Lutheran dispute, which began in 1527 by a Wittenberg professor, Agricola, has resulted in a term that has come to have both religious and secular meanings.

Atheism creates the most robust conception of antinomianism. "If there is no God, then everything is permitted." Both Dostoyevsky and Sartre demonstrated that this assertion is the inescapable result of atheism. Atheism has no moral absolutes. If everything is evolving, the need vanishes to assert that there must be a Creator or an Intelligent Designer (Darwin). But if everything is evolving, how can moral standards not also be evolving, too? With no God, humans become the final standard. But which humans? In the end, atheistic philosophy has no stopping point in its headlong rush into unbridled chaos. One needs to read only the news to see this demonstrated daily.

However, the antinomian dispute among Lutherans has a much narrower definition than that which is found in atheistic philosophy. In this theological case, some Lutheran teachers created an antinomian position for Christians by asserting that in the punctiliar event of justification the Law no longer had a place. However, in the ongoing process of sanctification, the Law was still useful. Justification, they said correctly, was by Christ alone. However, to avoid sanctification becoming a human work, both the role of Law and the definition of sin were revised in an attempt to maintain their ideas of both grace and of freedom.

Johannes Agricola, one of the Wittenberg professors to whom antinomianism is first attributed, began to teach, "If you sin, be happy, it should have no consequence." He taught that although non-Christians were under the Law, Christians were entirely free from it, being under the gospel alone. Sin was redefined as a mere malady or impurity rather than as a power that rendered the sinner guilty and damnable before God. The Law now has no role in repentance, repentance that was now caused instead by the knowledge of the love of God alone. In short, Lutheran antinomians insisted that faith alone guarantees eternal security in heaven, regardless of one's actions. This is also the antinomian definition of Christian freedom! Since the guarantee of eternal security is arguably

---

34. BAGD, s.v. "νόμος."

Luther's entire pastoral project in his greatest treatise *The Bondage of the Will*, the antinomian misapprehension of how this assurance and freedom is achieved is no small controversy!

Careful additional qualifications of the Lutheran antinomian position include these parts:

- They did argue that the Law could be preached in its third use, but only in the town hall, in the realm of its civil function (a modified first use).
- The Law could be preached as a positive demand to Christians.
- The Law could be preached in its positive essence, instructional sense, or educational content.
- They argued quite simply that the Law should not be preached in the church to Christians.[35]

Luther was forced, reluctantly, to enter into formal dispute with this teaching late in his career. Because this is the most mature Luther, it is also the most definitive description of his position. In the careful theses that he crafted in the five antinomian disputes he does not surrender his doctrine of Christian freedom from the Law.

To begin, Luther notes that antinomians attack the Reformation doctrine by "damning as a sacrilege, the terrifying of the pious by the Law."[36] He responds that even when teaching the Law "so as to admonish to the good," or "by way of exhortation, such admonishments and exhortations still condemn and are given because the Christian is still a sinner."[37] He is here pointing out that completely eliminating the condemning function of the Law from Christian ears misunderstands the actual current reality of unresurrected Christians. Unlike the antinomian teaching, Christians are and remain sinners. Christians are and remain in the flesh. Christian *consciences* are the battle ground between the condemning Law and the preaching of the Holy Spirit. Since the Law is given to reveal and expose sin and then to condemn it, it remains vital to preach it to believers who are currently and always struggling with sin until their resurrection. But the Law has to stay in its own lane. After the Law's rightful condemnation, it is finished. In the conscience, the gospel always has the last and definitive word. Luther says, "But when the Law

35. WA 39I:344.30.
36. WA 39I:497.24–25.
37. WA 39I:474.16.

is taught, the Gospel follows and sneaks in, saying: 'Listen, O Law, see to it lest you jump beyond your area and encloser.'"[38] Notice here that the gospel limits not merely the law's condemnation, but the Law *itself*.

> This is how those fanatics behave, that by means of the sacrament and Christ's example they do away with Christ himself. For if the law is done away with, there is no knowledge of what Christ is or what he has done, how he has fulfilled the law for us. For if I wish to understand the fulfilling of the law which is Christ, it is necessary to know what the law and its fulfillment are. This cannot be learned without teaching that the law is not fulfilled in us, and that we are thus guilty of sin and death. In the church, then, the teaching of the law is necessary and must be altogether retained, without which Christ cannot be retained. In sum, to do away with the law but to retain sin and death is to conceal the sickness of sin and death to men's ruination. If sin and death have been removed (as Christ has done) then [the Law] would happily be done away with, or I should rather say, would be upheld, as it says in Romans 3:31.[39]

This bring up the critical question, "Does the preaching of the Law as exhortation or admonition cause Christian good works?" Not according to Luther, in these theses from the fourth Antinomian Disputation:

35. "Indeed, only faith in Christ justifies, only it fulfills the Law, only it does good works *without the Law*.

36. "For only (faith) receives the forgiveness of sin and *spontaneously* does good works through love.

37. "It is true that after justification good works follow spontaneously *without the Law*, that is, *without it either helping or exhorting* any longer.

38. "In sum: the Law is neither useful nor necessary for justification *or for any good works*, let alone salvation."[40]

With such clarity, it defies all common sense that the third use of the Law got included in the official document called the Lutheran Confessions.

---

38. WA 39I:445.15–16.
39. LW 73:66.
40. LW 73:62; italics added.

One could add here Paul's clear word in his Letter to Titus that faith is surely not antinomian:

> But when the goodness and loving kindness of God our Savior appeared, he saved us, not because of deeds done by us in righteousness, but according to his own mercy, by the washing of regeneration and renewal of the Holy Spirit, whom he poured out upon us richly through Jesus Christ our Savior, so that we might be justified by his grace and becomes heirs in hope of eternal life. The saying is sure, and *I want you to insist on these things, so that those who have believed in God may be careful to apply themselves to good deeds*; these are excellent and profitable to men. (Titus 3:4–8; italics added)

Luther Versus Current Lutheran Orthodox Teaching

I. The Law Forever!

Lutheran orthodoxy teaches an abstraction of the Law called *lex aeterna* (eternal Law). They teach an imagined distinction between the Law's *essence* (God's good eternal will) and its current lesser *function* necessitated by sin (accusation). This false presupposition, an imagined distinction, allows the claim that the Law can be benign and friendly for the newly able Christian.

Robert Scaer is an eminent example among current Lutheran orthodox theologians. He treats the more libertine wings of the American denominations with their deserved disdain, opprobrium, and scorn. However, he falsely assumes that the proper solution to this desperate American church problem is—more Law! Together with other orthodox Lutherans, he calls for a reconsideration of the third use of the Law.[41]

It is truly amazing how far human theologians will go to try to evade the clear words of Paul's gospel in Rom 10:4: "Christ is the end of the law for righteousness for everyone who believes." Instead, from fear, the large majority of Christians cling to the false hope that they are now newly able to accomplish, or at least able to be successfully directed by, the Law's to-do list of demands. They propose the solution of the third use of the Law as that which will deliver from the false theology of antinomianism together with its libertinism.

---

41. Scaer, "Third Use of the Law."

But that is not the only motive for this reconsideration. After all, it is terrifying to cede complete control to Christ alone, because that requires us to acknowledge our helplessness and, by extension, forces us to rely upon God's promise and election alone. Paul insists that the correct hearing of the Law is abject terror. That is the required first step in salvation. It is required because, without the Law's insistent and non-escape accusation, we will maintain almost to the death some claim to self righteousness. Freed from the Law's insistent accusation by the gift of another righteousness, Christians can cheerfully acknowledge and agree with its clear and damning judgment, "that every mouth may be stopped and the whole world held accountable to God" (Rom 3:21). Freed Christians *are the only people on earth* who can agree cheerfully with the Law's damning accusation, solely because they have already been counted perfectly righteous in Christ. (This happens by promise, and not by Law as third users would have it.)

Antinomians and Lutheran orthodoxy despise each other, yet the two have a shared suspicion that the second use of the Law alone will not be able to point toward that which alone will produce the desired ethical behavior in Christians. Antinomians believe that the Law should not be preached to Christians in the church but only in the town hall. They think that the gospel alone should be able to produce righteous behavior. The orthodox, on the other hand, theologically do insist on the technical upholding of the second use, but in practice fear that the Law's insistent condemnation will depress Christian hearers. The result is that both are in favor of an optimistic third use, where the Law is a justified Christian's friend, albeit in different venues.

We come now to the philosophical mechanism Lutheran orthodox depends upon to make the Law into a Christian's friend. Lutheran orthodoxy evades the fact that *Christ is the end of the law* by creating this imagined distinction within the Law itself. Why? So that the Law can be carefully preserved, and go on forever and ever, even within the new kingdom of grace-righteousness-life. The newly created evasion works by making a distinction between the imagined *essence* (Latin *res*) of the Law as different from its imagined *lesser* function—its relentless judging accusation that exposes remaining sin.[42] Harnack, a nineteenth-century Lutheran theologian, thought he was being faithful to Luther's teaching

---

42 Hopman, "Luther's *Antinomian Disputations*."

in making this distinction. Amazingly, against both Paul and Luther, the great majority of Lutheran teachers agree with him.

Against this clever evasion are Luther's clear words in the *Antinomian Disputations*, where he refuses any such distinction. Instead, he says that one can always recognize Law by its *effect*. And its effect is the Law's sole God-given distinctive:

> The Law *is* the revelation of wrath, since repentance, at least insofar as it shows sin, and the revelation of wrath are effects of the Law. For even if we do not put down these letters, L-A-W, we are still looking *at the thing itself*. Fear of conscience *itself*, sadness *itself*, are transferred from letters and grammar into feeling and kill the heart. . . . We are not concerned about the word "Law" but about *the thing itself*.[43]

In vital contrast, Lutheran orthodoxy makes a distinction between the Law, in relation to God himself, which goes on forever and ever, as a contrast to and as a priority over the Law's attack against human's sin, which is only its function in this age. This eternal Law (*lex aeterna*) describes the eternal will of God, unrelated to humans. Such a will is good. This will of God always was and always will exist into eternity. This spiritually and good will of God only becomes accusatory when sin enters the picture. So the essence of the Law is the good eternal will of God, while its lesser function of accusation and judgment of sin is distinguished as only temporary in this passing age. Harnack and orthodoxy do distinguish the gospel from the Law, except that for them, the Law has merely a secondary, accidental, alien, condemning sense or office. When this happens, the proper distinction of Law and gospel is entirely subverted. The entire reason that Luther insisted upon that distinction in proclamation is that is serves one vital purpose—to close every single loophole or way forward, except to go to Christ.

A brief one-phrase definition of eternal Law is "Any concept of Law defined apart from sin and the Law's attack on sinners."

This distinction, which enables the Law to be understood as essentially good and not essentially accusatory, becomes the objective framework for a whole theological system that ends up subverting Reformation proclamation. It does so by proposing that the Law can be a positive commandment or directive, apart from its condemning function. To make this more palatable, the orthodox make an additional distinction.

---

43. *WA* 39I:415.13–416.3; italics added.

Justification is solely by Christ, without the Law. But sanctification, on the other hand, is an effort where Christians participate and can be directed by their newly made friend. *Participate* may be an effort to avoid saying *cooperate*, but it is the same thing—namely, a human righteousness project.

But this has predictably disastrous effects on proclamation! With this false presupposition in place, proclamation inevitably becomes a how-to lecture regarding the necessary achievement of certain moral imperatives. In turn, the active subjects are we, we, we. Jesus, while always implicit, mainly has his work serve as an example. The second use of the Law, with its God-given condemnation meant to drive us to Christ alone, is characterized by these theologians as worm theology. They accuse such preaching as falsely depressing the newly athletic and able Christian. *Luther disapproves*: "They damn as sacrilege the terrifying of the pious by the Law."[44]

> The essence of the law, for Luther, is its condemning office. Luther here shows that the law is always related to sin. The *term* "law" can be removed, but wherever sin is revealed there *is* the law "in the most proper sense." This leaves no room for an essence of the law that would possibly be law "in the most proper sense" apart from its condemnation of sin.... This is not a passing argument for Luther in the *Antinomian Disputations*, but one that is consistently and often repeated. For Luther, law and sin cannot be separated: "These three—law, sin and death are inseparable."[45]

Nicholas Hopman, in an extensive article titled "Luther's *Antinomian Disputations* and *lex aeterna*," concludes,

> While the law must be proclaimed, precisely in order to kill, time must also be taken in the old creation to announce that Christ and Christians are "*sine lege*" (without the law) as Luther's example shows. Not only is this the proper teaching of justification but also good works are done only "without the law." This means that the preacher need not fear the freedom of the gospel and look for some kind of eternal third use of the law with which to tame the gospel.[46]

---

44. *WA* 39I:497; see also Rom 5:20.
45. Hopman, "Luther's *Antinomian Disputations*," 154.
46. Hopman, "Luther's *Antinomian Disputations*," 172.

In the second set of *Antinomian Disputations* Luther literally defines the Law's very being (its *essence*) as synonymous with its office, and certainly not distinguished from it:

18. "Whatever shows sin, wrath, and death exercises the *office* [italics added] of the Law, be it in the Old or in the New Testament.

19. "For to reveal sin is nothing else—nor can it be anything else—than to be Law, in *fact* (*esse legem*) or to be the *effect* [italics added] and power of the Law in the most proper sense (*Propriissimam*)."[47]

Again Luther writes,

> When we speak of the Law, we speak about the Law's proper *effect* [italics added], which it can have or perform in this corrupt nature. Besides, we all experience that it can work nothing but despair. . . . For by itself the Law cannot do anything but afflict, ruin, and agitate consciences. These are matters we speak of whenever the Law is mentioned . . . when one treats the Law, then one treats the nature and the power and effect of the Law . . . you always ought to remain in the chief (*principali*) definition of the Law, that it works wrath and hatred and despair.[48]

For Luther there is no distinction between the Law's requirement and the Law's accusation. Proclamation under this correct presupposition begins always with the needed word of Law. This happens when the proclaimer asks from the text for the day: "What does this word expose regarding either our sin or our human need? And what makes this requirement impossible for us to fulfill it?" Only then follows the gospel, that Jesus has already done this for you. The condemnation stops for the Christian only when one hears the promise. The nonintuitive promise is that God loves *sinners*, (not the "newly morally athletic") and that they qualify! When the good news of the cross has been heard and believed, the demand of the Law ceases with it. This is how the Law is to be preached to Christians as fulfilled, not as needing to be fulfilled by them. This is how the vital second use of the Law functions properly. This is true Christian proclamation and not lecture. When one believes that we are saved by the righteousness *of* Jesus, then every third use is rendered useless and void. The Law is now placed *behind* the Christian, not in front of him.

---

47. WA 39I:157.
48. WA 39I:445.5-14, 446.5-6.

The Law itself ceases formally when what the Law demands is done in us, and we render it freely and willingly, not because the Law demands it, but out of righteousness and of goodness and of God himself. The Law is *empty* because it does not have anything to demand or accuse of (*exigat aut arguat*), since "they do by their nature what the Law requires (Rom. 2:14)."[49]

II. Argument Against the *lex aeterna*, the Orthodox Presupposition

A strong argument can be made that the most fundamental *res* of the Law is defined neither as *the good, eternal will of God* nor its *function as God's relentless attack on human sin*. Rather, even more fundamentally than these two, its *res* is that the Law is *ostensive*. The Law's whole nature is fundamentally ostensive. That is, it is meant to point beyond itself to Someone else.

Case one: Adam and Eve. When the serpent said that if they ate the fruit their eyes would be opened and that they would be like God, knowing good and evil, they discovered that when their eyes were opened, they did indeed know evil and that there was a good, but that they no longer knew what the good was. The good is no simple thing! Only God determines what is the good, but since they were now cut off from intimate communion with God, they now had to approximate or guess at what the good now was. Fast forward to current humanity and we find ourselves in the precise same predicament. Yes, God has in the meantime revealed his Law, but the Law is merely ostensive. Like a Dead End or No Outlet sign is ostensive to the driver saying, "Not this way," but *without any further helpful direction*. The Law is sent only to point away from itself to another. *It is limited to telling us what the not-good is; or if it does describe the good in a general way, it cannot get us there!* While helpful in warning, it is not helpful in the solution to our problem. The problem lies not with the holy content that the Law expresses. Rather the problem is that the Law has nothing to work with. The Law cannot produce any described holiness, because such an outcome is rendered impossible by our fallen fleshly nature.

Inevitably, without Christ, even the very best of humanity use the Law for the wrong purpose! We use the Law to endlessly approximate the

---

49. WA 39I:434.19–435.4.

good without any success. Witness the endless rows of legal volumes with case law seeking to approximate the good. Witness the entire judiciary enterprise that only promises a *chance* at the good and right outcome. Witness the abject (and mysterious) failure of all morality and idealism.

Case two: The gospel with its promise. God gave the Law to direct us, to *point us* to Christ. When Christ arrives, the Law ends. Its ostensive *res* has been fulfilled. When the Law has finally accomplished and completed its purpose of directing us to Christ, it *ends*. Christ is the meaning of the Law. If Christ rules the conscience, there is no Law. Wherever Christ is, there is no Law. We are categorically freed from its condemnation (Rom 8:1). In heaven, says Luther, the saints need no Law, so in that place the Law is *vacua*, emptied. But in the life to come it will be completely removed.[50]

If the Law is merely ostensive, it certainly cannot be described as eternal in any useful sense. Jesus, in John 6:28–29, is crystal clear. The Pharisees ask, "What must we do, to be doing the works of God?" As noted previously, Jesus corrects their short question *three* ways! "This is the *work, of God*, that you *believe in him* whom he has sent" (italics added). Faith, not Law as the subject and director. No eternal Law here! Although the issue presented here is works, and by extension obedience, the implicit question is, "If not the Law, how shall we know what works to do?" In fact, Jesus's answer has no Law at all! Just faith, and Jesus, and his righteousness. So, in effect, Jesus is preaching, "When I appear, the Law ends."

Paul agrees. He is similarly categorical about this in Romans, leaving absolutely no room for alternate eternal views created for the purpose of sustaining the false hope that the Law can be good (and a friend) to the newly able. In contrast, Paul states the sentence that mercifully (and categorically) kills that false hope: "Christ is the *end* of the Law for righteousness for all who believe" (Rom 10:4; italics added).

The Greek word for "end" is *telos*. The Greek is far richer and more nuanced in meaning than the English "end": (1) *Telos* has a *time* characteristic, suggesting the completion of a process. (2) *Telos* has a *goal* characteristic, suggesting the main controlling purpose. And (3) *Telos* has a *conclusion* characteristic, noting complete cessation.[51]

---

50. *LW* 73:80.
51. BAGD, s.v. "τέλος."

Therefore, the accusation against Paul, articulated by his opponents in 2 Corinthians, that Paul teaches that all things are lawful (from which Paul does not back down!) suddenly makes sense. It is not that Christians are anarchists or antinomian, but rather that where Christ lives, there the Law ends. Where there is no Law, there is therefore no more sin, and where there is no more sin, there is no more death. "The sting of death is sin, and the power of sin is the law. But thanks be to God, who gives us the victory through our Lord Jesus Christ" (1 Cor 15:56–57). This expresses Paul's exact thesis (Rom 5:20–21) that there are two opposing kingdoms competing within the Christian—Law-sin-death versus grace-righteousness-life. Each component part of these kingdoms corresponds exactly to the other, and each absolutely annihilates the other. So, when Christ reveals that the good *is the righteousness of Jesus* (Rom 3:21–22; Gal 2:16; Phil 3:9), then our eyes are finally opened, by the Holy Spirit, to see and to walk, by faith, within the only thing that is the good.

A Christian can delight in the Law, because it is now behind him and not in front of him. Our righteousness is completed because we have Christ. "It is no longer I who live, but Christ who lives in me, and the life I now live in the flesh, I live by faith in the one who loved me and gave himself for me" (Gal 2:20). Christ is the fulfillment of the Law—what the Law was pointing to and directing us to all the time.

Summary: The second use of the Law, understood properly and scripturally, is understanding that the Law's essence *is* its ostensiveness. That is, it was given most essentially to point us to Christ. Only when it has deposited us there has the Law's essence been completed. Such an understanding of the second use absolutely precludes a proposed third use. Additionally, any attempt at a third use reveals a Pharisaical *misuse* of the Law's God-given purpose, which repeats and expresses the original sin itself—an attempt to be like God.

III. Is the Third Use of the Law Implicit in Luther's Theology?

Because Lutheran orthodoxy cannot deny the clarity of Luther's words listed from the Galatians commentary, they say that the third use of the Law is still *implicit* in instances of Luther's teaching, such as in his treatise on vocation and in the Small Catechism.

In Luther's treatise on Christian vocation, the vital question arises concerning the specific quality that make a good work *good*. This treatise asserts, with Paul, that it is only *faith* that makes a work good. The Medieval church basically taught that holy orders, with their attempted separation from the sinful world, were necessary to create good works, while the rest of the "unwashed" population languished in comparative unholiness. Luther, by contrast, asserts that a mother and father, who by faith live out their calling in the office of parenthood, and *believe* that such an office is not only God-commanded but God-pleasing and holy, are doing good works. In the Large Catechism, Luther states that such a commandment locates the *venue of blessing*:

> See, this work is well pleasing to my God in heaven; this I know for certain. . . . O how great a price all the Carthusian monks and nuns would pay if in the exercise of their religion they could bring before God a single work done in accordance with his commandment and could say with a joyful heart in his presence, "Now I know that this work is well pleasing to Thee!"[52]

But isn't this a case in Luther in which the Law is directive? First, Luther's point lies elsewhere. Their faith that performing their daily office of parenthood has God's word of command is that which makes it a good work, while the celibacy and the humanly imposed rigor of the holy orders do not have any such word. Faith in the word of God is the essence of what makes their day-to-day service a good work. So only the one who has faith in God's word has God's blessing. And no, the Law is not directive here. What it does is merely ostensive. It can indicate the region of what lies under God's blessing, but it lacks the power to get us into that venue of blessing, even for a Christian! Even if it could, the Law is unable to detail for parents what constitutes the shape of the correct relationship to each unique child, to each other, and to the varied household responsibilities. Neither the commandment on honoring parents, nor the commandment forbidding adultery, have any useful positive directive function. They merely point to what is out of bounds. The Law can always point away from itself to the place where God's blessing lies. However, it can neither get us there, nor can it provide the detail required to be helpfully directive of our behavior. The claim that Luther is here implicitly using a third use of the Law is thus demonstrably false. In Luther's Catechisms, the Law remains accusatory, diagnostic, and ostensive, but not directive.

---

52. Tappert, *Book of Concord*, 381.

Continuing their argument that the third use is implicit in Luther's writings, Pietists and Lutheran orthodox cite the bipartite structure of Luther's negative-positive explanations of the Ten Commandments in the Small Catechism, which seem to have a directive function rather than being limited to an accusatory function. Although the explanation for the first commandment, "We should fear, love and trust in God above all things" is not possible to humanly perform, the other explanations have both positive and negative formulations. For instance, the commandment on the Lord's name says negatively that "we should fear and love God so that we do not curse, swear, practice magic, lie, or deceive by his name." But then positively it continues, "but in every time of need call on him, pray to him, praise him, and give him thanks."[53] Is not the last positive part clearly doable? Surely, this must represent an implicit third use of the Law! Does not Luther here provide a directive function for the Law? (All the following explanations follow a similar pattern of a list of what not to do followed by a list of what to do.)

To deny this in another way, it is only necessary to enlarge upon an additional theological point regarding the Law's limitation to being merely ostensive. One could add that Luther made no distinction, anywhere, between the Law's *requirement* and the Law's *accusation*. The positive parts of his commandment explanations are still performative *requirements*. Requirements are always going to end in accusation for the sinner because the Law is all or nothing in its demands. Every human, even the best Christian, will eventually be forced to concede under the Law's thunder that "I cannot perform perfectly, therefore I am condemned as accused." Luther is writing all these meanings, not as abstract lectures to everybody, but, rather, specifically to Christians, who understand that they are *simul justus et peccator*—100 percent sinner and 100 percent righteous at the same time. And sinner a Christian remains, even though 100 percent righteous at the same time. Reformation Christians will not hear these catechism meanings as implicitly directive, but as Luther meant them—describing what happens only when one is in Christ. Only Christians know that there is no refuge for a sinner in creating the forlorn hope of improved performance. The cross of Jesus and his blood that secured a new covenant of his righteousness cannot be combined with any form of human righteousness with its claimed improvement. Luther's axiom still stands: *lex semper accusat*—the Law always accuses.

---

53. Tappert, *Book of Concord*, 342.

CHAPTER 9

Allure and the Necessity of Threat

You are not a free agent. You are captured by the allure, the attraction of the one God or the other god. Luther famously said in his treatise *Bondage of the Will* that "you are a horse that is ridden."[1] Heiko Obermann carefully titled his narrative of the reformer's life *Man Between God and the Devil*. As little as the moon can break away from the gravitational pull of the earth, or the earth break away from the gravitational pull of the sun, so little can you change your orbit around your controlling master. When Christ breaks in to set us free, only then can we talk of freedom. Scripture alone reveals to us our utter blindness to this fact, and our abject and complete human inability to ever escape our bondage to the powers of Law-sin-death. Only when that unique scriptural presupposition completely overtakes and informs our understanding does the whole Bible text make perfect sense.

As one instance of this, it then makes perfect sense that there are only two kinds of people in the world—those who are held by the allure used by the evil one, who attracts and ensnares them by the lure of such things as power, greed, pleasure, or recognition. This group is in utter contrast to those who are freed to follow the allure of the other master, the One who loves them, Jesus Christ.

By definition, to qualify as a god there must be an operative irresistible attractive allure. But why is it that the devil has such a powerful attraction upon us that only Christ can break it? That is not explained. We simply experience it as fact. It is a fact made blindingly obvious to us in our inability to escape the thrall of the allure that the evil one has over us. Even pagan philosophers acknowledge our human predicament, that *knowing* the morally right thing does not give us the *power to perform* the good thing (see also Rom 7:21–24).

1. *LW* 33:65.

There are at least two things mysterious about the devil's allure, called temptation:

- It even affected Jesus! He battled against temptation every moment he lived among us. Paul says that this is because when Jesus was incarnate, he also took upon himself this thing called the flesh, a venue or inherent weakness that evidently gives regnant power to the opposing kingdom. Paul writes, "For the law of the Spirit of life has set you free in Christ Jesus from the law of sin and death. For God has done what the law, weakened by the flesh, could not do. By sending his own Son in the likeness of sinful flesh and for sin he condemned sin in the flesh, in order that the righteous requirement of the law might be fulfilled in us, who walk not according to the flesh but according to the Spirit" (Rom 8:2–4). The book of Hebrews says about Jesus that he was tempted in every way that we are, yet without sin (Heb 4:15). The Bible doesn't give us the explanation for the allure or attraction of evil, it simply says that it's there and that it has to be dealt with by every one of us. Jesus had to deal with it, and his overcoming it, while in the flesh, is part of our salvation.

- The second puzzling thing about the devil's allure is how limited the evil one is by way of competition with God. In the once rare field of demon possession, one is impressed immediately with how opposite these two opponents are. If God deals in light and truth, the devil is limited to their opposite, darkness and lies. If God creates beauty, then the devil is limited to ugliness. If God gives life, the devil can only give death. If holiness is attended by a lightness and joy and sometimes even by a beautiful smell, then those who belong to the devil always have a heaviness and gloom or despair about them. Death in particular it distinguished by its awful smell. But, if that is so, how then is the devil able to attract anyone, limited as he is to work with this handicap? Without a comprehensive answer, we may know at least this for sure, that he does it by lying and covering up where such obedience to his allure is leading. "Just live for the moment," he whispers, "live for yourself. Don't think about the consequences." The entire operation of the evil one is controlled by deception, by the power of death wearing a mask.

Logical outcomes that follow from this assessment of the human predicament include the following:

1) In Romans, Paul portrays sin as a personal phenomenon, a god, within. I agree with the British theologian N. T. Wright, who makes this assertion in his commentary on the book of Romans.[2] If so, the destructive allure of evil is an attraction from which we cannot escape. It can only be resisted, never defeated completely. What is more, that assertion describes our entire situation, the complete context of our life here in the age of the fall. It is the reason why Paul in Rom 5, and the whole of 1 Peter, tells Christians not to be surprised by their suffering, but to hold on to their hope—thus describing, along with Revelation, that the whole of Christian experience is a living in the tension between suffering (caused by the predacious allure of the evil one) and hope (the allure of Christ).[3]

2) Success can never be the proper category to characterize Christian hope, nor a controlling strategy to describe Christian attempts to deal with this mysterious destructive allure. Those who participated in the resistance movements against the suffocating Nazi regime said success could never have been their primary motivation. First, the regime was just too monolithic. Second, the risks that attended resistance (personal torture and death, and the same for their families) so far outweighed the putative advantage of, say, the pathetically small gestures of distributing mimeographed fliers that it rendered any such resistance clearly unreasonable if not almost insane. Because of this, the majority did not resist. Yet even puny resistance was constantly engaged by some, refusing to consider the relative effect of their resistance. They could not weigh success against the risk because, they said, *resistance was the only way to stay morally sane*. Thus, *the power to resist* alone is our warrant for believing that we are rescued, and that we are the new creation, the children of God (Rom 8:12–17). The power to resist is what John means when he says, "You have overcome the evil one" (1 John 2: 14). On the contrary, success may more accurately describe the predacious ruling authority that the word of God allows the beast to exercise against the saints during this age of the fall (Rev 13:7). Thus, every Christian effort to witness, which is informed by calculations about effectiveness, progress, approval, acclaim or any of the varieties of success, openly imitates the beast. Moreover, practicing such

---

2. Wright, "Romans," 525.
3. Beker, *Suffering and Hope*.

calculation before risking any putative witness shows the saints' profound doubt in the efficacy of the resurrection and the activity of the judgment of the word of God. So, the saints—attempting vainly to forestall or obviate defeat—are defeated anyway, ignominiously.[4] Expecting or insisting upon success is impertinent to the promise of the gospel! Yet the promise of the gospel is no melancholy message! It authorizes realistic hope for the saints, who through their vocation of preaching (advocacy) confront the full and awesome militancy of the power of death incarnate in the ruling principalities of the world, nourishing patience for the judgment of the word of God and, meanwhile, trusting nothing else at all.[5]

3) The relation between God's allure and the diametrically opposed remaining allure of the sin within our flesh is not an all-or-nothing control that one would expect of the planetary metaphor. This would imply that triumph over all tension in this era was a possibility. Unfortunately, this seems to be the paradigm assumed by and characterizing much American preaching. However, the relation between the two, within a Christian, is experienced as both an *irresolvable and an inescapable tension* between the two most powerfully opposed persons/forces in the cosmos. Both allures continue to act upon each Christian so long as one live in the age of the fall. Thus the categories to describe our Christian experience in the New Testament—*suffering* and *hope*—are words that describe this tension that is so irresolvable. One cannot escape into either side of the tension. Non-Christians do not experience this tension, since they are completely sold under a false god (Rom 6:12ff, esp. v. 20).

4) Therefore, preaching that explicitly or implicitly creates the false expectation among Christians that a saved life should certainly be more victorious, triumphant, or tension–free than what their personal life is currently exhibiting is not only preaching false hope but creating further torment for Christ's sheep.

5) Possession, as a category describing the human predicament, describes the complete erosion of the *human will* to resist. The final stages of any addiction demonstrate this phenomenon. The first step of the AA twelve-step program accurately describes it. In this situation, the human being has ceded/lost complete control over his or

---

4. Stringfellow, *Conscience & Obedience*, 111.
5. Stringfellow, *Conscience & Obedience*, 112.

her life to another personal power, who is crushing the last vestiges of their very life. Rescue is thus defined as having a higher personal power take over their existence in the body. The foundational revelation from this experience is that we are not our own lords, nor are we free agents. Many, many Christians do not get this far in their theology, which in AA is the first step! Any AA person who has only pretended that they have yielded to God's power is absolutely not rescued. They continue in their enslavement to the destructive power that will surely kill them. For them, any and all attempts at further steps in the program are rendered pointless.

6) Conversion, as a category describing human rescue from the allure of the evil one, shares this salient feature of the phenomenon of possession in that God always finds a will that is captivated when he begins our rescue. If that is so, then by definition the will cannot respond to the offer of salvation, and all preaching directed to the will of man so as to produce a decision for Christ is not only woefully misguided but biblically obtuse. Such an approach cannot be made congruent, consistent, or consonant with any of the biblical narratives of conversion or, for that matter, with any of the sermon patterns (the kerygma) that make up 28 percent of the book of Acts, and that serve as the foundational narrative for our Christian creeds. But if the captivated human will is not a possible target for preaching ("Make a decision for Christ!"), then what is? Luther calls it *the conscience*—the human juridical capacity to know that the final verdict over our life rests with another. Thus, the juridical category of righteousness, and how to achieve righteousness, is the controlling theme in both Old and New Testament. Preaching then becomes simply the proclamation by a higher authority, to the conscience, that right standing before God has been achieved by the completed historical act of Jesus's death on the cross and his resurrection from death. In that event, the required righteousness has been accomplished completely, once for all. Further, this righteousness is proclaimed as counted to the hearer who believes. Only such announcement—

- that saving righteousness has to belong to another,
- and has to be given as a sheer gift (grace),
- and properly is received by faith alone—

only this proclamation is able to create a quiet conscience, secure from all accusations of the evil one. Proper Christian confidence is founded upon the fact that all this must be achieved within God's agency alone. Any human-divine partnership here ("You must accept Jesus") would create an uncertain calculus over whether *I* had accepted warmly enough, on my part. Additionally, believing the gospel—that God's only Son has done for us what we could not do for ourselves—is not an act of the will (no phrase resembling *accepting Jesus* is found anywhere in Scripture!) but a miracle created by God's Holy Spirit. Christian preaching has this distinctive: that it believes that God alone will create the miracle of faith, when and where he chooses. Thus, the effectiveness of preaching rests completely with whether it is God's word and not ours. To expect conversion without attending carefully to whether one brings God's actual word is a blasphemous assertion of human pride.

7) The case of exorcism reveals the proper function of the Law by exposing the falsehood of the claim that the Law has a third function. First, only two fundamental laws collide in the event of exorcism—the Law of Christ, which Paul describes as grace-righteousness-life versus the Law of Law-sin-death. Also, two *pairs* of persons meet in direct conflict: the exorcist meets the spirit-bound one, and, through them, the person of Jesus meets the personal evil one in direct conflict. Several unique things happen when these two mortally opposed warring powers meet. First, human speech has two moods—the declarative and the imperative. What transpires in the event of exorcism is that the exorcist, who is used to the declarative mood that attends most sermons, finds that his speech necessarily changes to the imperative mood. The exorcist *commands*. For here the Law of Christ collides with the Law of Law-sin-death over who shall triumph. Second, the exorcist is made painfully aware that he or she is a sinner, in the flesh, completely naked, whose secrets and faults are all known by the opposing evil one. Therefore, the exorcist also is forced to rely upon faith alone, that he or she stands only by virtue of the Holy Spirit's covering of another's righteousness. To enter this combat trusting in human righteousness is madness! Third, the warrant for any command in this combat is that the blood of Jesus has erased any false claim of the evil one upon this possessed person. I do not know why the blood of Jesus is so central in this

combat, but it surely redirects one's attention to its central role in the New Testament witness. Finally, the exorcist commands to know the name of the evil one in question. Then, by the opposing name of Jesus it is summarily driven out. Notably, the case of exorcism reveals centrally what Paul means by his phrase "the Law of Christ." The Law of Christ is the power of the entire kingdom of grace-righteousness-life in active combat with the tyranny of Law-sin-death.

8) If, as the Bible so often reveals, evil is never accurately or adequately treated as a mere abstraction, but requires also to be considered as a personal entity (see the implicit argument of Rom 1–8), then the primary way to discuss evil is to speak of evil *ones*, as we pray in the Lord's Prayer: deliver us from the evil *one* (Matt 6:13). This, in turn, reveals that the whole of salvation is the narrative of mortal combat in which we find ourselves—a combat that is being engaged by two opposed persons. In this combat, which takes the form Christians experiencing temptation by evil ones, every square inch, every split second is claimed and counter-claimed by these two opponents. Thus, for example, to deny such hymns as "Onward, Christian Soldiers"[6] any place in some modern hymnals on the basis that they are hopelessly outdated and embarrassingly and inappropriately martial merely betrays incomprehensible biblical ignorance.

9) The *personal character of the two opponents is taken on by those who serve them*. So, if evil is personal, then the goal of salvation must be *the restoration of the person/personality* so affected (to become like Christ), while the goal of temptation is always the diminution and final destruction of the person/personality. The latter every living person can attest to by their own experience.

10) *Our sin has to be revealed to us!* It is not self evident. Our bondage to a false god entails not only perversion of the will but also blindness of our intellect (see both John 9 and Luther's Heidelberg Disputation). Worst of all, our bondage consists fundamentally in our conviction that we are free! (So the Jews of John 8:33). This is what is denoted everywhere, and this, alone, explains why Jesus is preached as the light of the world. The competing claim that the "objective" scientific method has become the light of the world through triumphing over previous, benighted "superstition" was summed up

---

6. Baring-Gould, "Onward, Christian Soldiers."

by its proud philosophers proudly calling the whole movement "The Enlightenment." Yet, all of our attempts to assume functions that belong to God alone entail benightedly false theological assertions regarding our definitions both of what God is and what God is not. Since God and humanity are related by *contradiction* (thus Luther in appendix II), the very acts we consider most holy are very likely the very worst sins. In John 1:9–11 and through the entire book of Mark, our unredeemed actions only demonstrate our continued failure to recognize God himself among us. This results inevitably in the crucifixion. The entire warrant for the crucifixion rested upon our theological assertion that Jesus's claim to be God was blasphemy. That most definitive event in history reveals that our humanity characteristically credits God's truth for a lie.

11) The story we are each living through is an exodus just like Israel's first exodus from slavery into the wilderness. Like them, we are embarked upon a dangerous journey through a hostile wilderness toward the promised land. The book of Romans plots our location as post-baptism (after crossing the water), surrounded by danger and hostile forces in the wilderness, led by the Spirit (now not a pillar of cloud or fire, but within us), journeying toward the promised land.

12) *The allure of the God who loves us is called the Holy Spirit.* Those who have tasted how good the love of God is, that he calls only sinners, that we all qualify, and how he makes us feel like we are home at last, and how this is the only true joy to be had, and how he fills us with true peace and love—this we tell each other by personal stories.

13) These stories (Christian personal witness) find their validation and confirmation in two ways: first, we understand by the testimony of our own hearts that what we are hearing from another Christian is true (often we have experienced the very same thing!); and second, by extension of that phenomenon, we know that the same Spirit is testifying in our two hearts to create the same unified conviction. Thus, we are united as brothers and sisters not only because we are all children of God, but we are united by a common Spirit who knits us all together in common conviction. Jesus was not ashamed to say that the whole objective of his suffering death and resurrection was so that we could have this Spirit, whose allure, and leading, and

comfort in suffering can now be turned loose in us who are his children (John 14, 15, 16).

14) Is grace irresistible? From the opponent's point of view, at least, it must be. Otherwise, Jesus's words of condemnation to the faculty at Jerusalem in John 10, "You do not believe because you are not of my flock," would make no sense. The absolute separation is here made, not based upon human volition, but upon God's foreknowledge. Only those who were foreknown demonstrate that by their belief in Jesus. Grace, regarded narrowly in its function as the initiatory action of God, also must be somehow irresistibly attractive or alluring. Paul would not be so surprised by grace, nor would it have become the controlling theme of his writing and preaching, had grace not overcome his own most willful opposition ("Saul, Saul, why do you kick against the goads?" [Acts 26:14]). Yet he is also capable of saying, "I was not disobedient to the heavenly vision" (v. 19). Thus, post-conversion, there is some place to talk about human volition, indeed, to assert that it exists here for the first time. For this reason also, the overly mechanical "once saved always saved" formulation is rejected by most Christian doctrine as incongruent to both scriptural witness and Christian experience.

In summary, two opposing conclusions regarding the threat of the Law and the allure of the Holy Spirit occur in the conflict between Paul and Luther versus the Pietists. In the first conclusion, the Pietists insist that the Law has now become benign and can serve a directive function because the Holy Spirit now enables a cooperation or a participation with the Law in the process of sanctification. Yes, the Law has been fulfilled for Christians in justification. But that does not justify the claim that the Law is no longer fearful. *So, for Pietists, the Law continues forever.* On the other hand, both Paul and Luther declare that such imagined cooperation is the very definition of the attempt at human righteousness, a beast from whose everlasting partial nature Jesus's righteousness delivers us. Jesus's righteousness and human righteousness annihilate each other. Paul and Luther's considered emphasis is that the Law will always be an accusatory threat to our flesh, and never a directive friend, even for the Spirit-filled Christian. So, in contrast to Pietism, Paul and Luther proclaim that *Christian freedom is only possible with the utter end of the Law.*

In the second place, Paul and Luther both insist upon the Law's proper location. Pietists believe that the allure of the Holy Spirit will enable one to now keep the Law. That is, Christians can retain it and keep it, without threat because of justification, now as a friend and director. That presupposition locates the Law and its function, finally, work helpfully *post justification*. Paul and Luther, on the other hand, insist that the threat of the Law never ends, even for a Christian. So, the "end of the Law" (Rom 10:4) is necessary and has to be literal in every syllable. That is, there is no more Law for those who are in Christ Jesus. We are freed. We are delivered from the Law's tyranny in our conscience. In this proclamation, the placement of the Law is confined to the flesh where it reveals our failures. The threat of the Law only becomes salutary when it drives the conscience to find its hope in Christ's righteousness alone. So the Law is restricted to being *always preparatory to faith*. When it seeks to rule in the conscience, the Reformation Christian dismisses it from the conscience after faith arrives. That is the gift bequeathed to us from the Reformation in Luther's rediscovery of Paul's gospel.

But how rarely this gift is proclaimed!

CHAPTER 10

Justifying God

Unique to the Gospel of Luke is this arresting sentence: "The tax collectors justified God" (Luke 7:29). But what could cause that amazing report? What is going on here? Previous to this strange and unexpected acclamation, the tax collectors had to have heard Jesus's crushing verdict over their lives. They were all made to hear, by Jesus's preaching, that they were guilty of cynical and self-serving practices in their lawfully authorized profession. They practiced their thievery under the color of Law, no less! So, under any just Law, they were without excuse, guilty, and justly hated by the entire populace. Jesus, in his preaching of the Law, delivered the only crushing verdict possible: guilty! So why would tax collectors, of all people, justify God?

The only explanation possible to this unexpected outcome is that they also heard Jesus proclaim something else, which accompanied that verdict. What followed that verdict of Law had to have been Jesus preaching the unexpected word of life, saying in effect: "God loves sinners! You qualify!" *Only people who have been freed from the Law's accusation are able to justify God's righteous verdict over all humanity: "You are a sinner!"* Absent the gospel, we will find forgiveness impossible, we will always defend ourselves, we will deny our sin, and we will blame others. However, people freed by the gospel gladly and without reservation declare that God is, and always was, righteous in his judgments.

The point here, and the point of this whole chapter is that *God's love always arrives first as accusation*. Luther said it this way: "God always has to be your devil before He can be your savior."[1] Nor does this process ever stop. Each day, a Christian stands accused. Yet, each day, a Christian also stands completely justified, rescued, and loved as God's own child, with whom he is well pleased. Every day, the battle goes on in the conscience

---

1. *LW* 33:62.

over which word will be the final word. Will it be the Law? Will it be the promise? (Because God's word is one undivided word, even though it comes as two events.) The Christian is given the responsibility of faith. That is, a Christian has the adult responsibility of hearing and claiming by faith the *gospel promise as the last word*.

> Peace with God means, in the same breath, war with the self and strife in the world. There is no "yes" to God without an accompanying "no" to the self, and likewise no "no" to the self without a "yes" to God. True faith has to do with being confronted with Another who makes us relinquish our own calculations and thoughts, wishes and hopes, and who breaks into our lives as a foreign reality, insisting that we recognize him as such. . . . *Thus, wherever God's Word meets us, it meets us as the enemy.*[2]

> For he who is in God's grace does what is pleasing to God. Therefore, he soon displeases the devil, the world, and his own flesh, and as long as he is righteous in the sight of God, he is a sinner to his flesh and to the world. Thus, war breaks out—war on the outside, but peace within—within, I say, not in a way that can be felt and pleasurably experienced with the senses, at least not always, but in an invisible way and through faith. For the peace of God passes all understanding (Phil 4:7); that is, it cannot be comprehended except through faith.[3]

Luther, in the forgoing citation, describes how peace is brought to what he calls the established conscience. There can be no established conscience without the utter cessation of the Law's rightful accusation. But God brings that accusation! Only those who have heard the whole gospel, which attends that judgment, and who know that they stand within Another's righteousness, are enabled by faith to say, "God, your judgment upon me is both right and righteous." But that struggle of faith for peace in the conscience is a continuing dynamic. Peace with God is won through to by never-ending conflict with unbelief and the lies of the evil one. Peace with God is only possible through hearing and claiming by faith that God is faithful in maintaining that Jesus is the last Word, and that he has the last word over us.

The God-given function of the Law is to root out our noxious security, to root out the beast called human righteousness. The diabolical

---

2. Iwand, *Righteousness of Faith*, 22; italics added.
3. *LW* 27:170.

despair of Satan seeks to make us despair of Christ by hearing the Law as the last word. But the gospel's despair is something entirely different. The gospel uses the Law the way every doctor uses an antidote to combat disease. The noxious security we seek to create by the dream of human righteousness so deeply inheres in all of us that it can be terrified out of us and despaired of only by the thunder of the righteous Law of God. "Evangelical despair, to which the Law should drive [one], is neither harmful nor does it abide, but prepares for conceiving faith in Christ, as it is written: to the poor the Gospel is preached."[4]

Gerhard Forde has noted that in this interplay between God's accusation and God's promise, it is proclamation that does the deed. Neither the Law nor the gospel are abstractions in this contest for peace in the conscience. As they are proclaimed, each of these words of God acts to accomplish in real time what God sent his word to do.

> The move is from the *language of being* to the *language of act*. The permanent change that the incarnation, death, and resurrection of Christ brings is to place this age under its eschatological end (telos).... [The preacher] *does* God, *does* the end and the new beginning to us.... His is the story of *God for us*.[5]

Ministry is first and foremost the ministry of proclamation, the concrete speaking of the Word of God, the doing of the sacramental deed, in the living present. The primary paradigm for ministry is absolution—concrete, present tense, I-to-you declaration in Word and sacrament authorized by the triune God: "I declare unto you the gracious forgiveness of all your sins in the name of the Father, the Son, and the Holy Spirit." That is the culmination of all we have been saying. *Ministry is the actual doing of the deed*.[6]

Ministry is doing the deed of election here and now, publicizing the mystery in and through the church. It has to do with the concrete, present-tense, public doing of the deed. Everything has been accomplished in Christ, so that this is now to be done.[7]

---

4. WA 39I:430.19.
5. Forde, *Theology Is for Proclamation*, 177; italics added.
6. Forde, *Theology Is for Proclamation*, 179; italics added.
7. Forde, *Theology Is for Proclamation*, 180.

Whoever becomes a believer becomes so through experiencing the action of God's word upon his conscience, which is done to him through his ears. The faith there engendered survives the righteous and terrifying verdict of Law and now justifies that very verdict, because the hearer has also been given, in the same proclamation, the last sure word, the word of promise.

Chapter 11

Ethics Renewed: Freed to Resist

Two Examples of Christian Freedom

ONLY THE FREED CAN resist. Our ability to resist is the primary evidence of our rescue from slavery. Paul says that we are free from sin. That is not the same as saying that we are sinless. Dreaming of such success is impertinent to the gospel. Our freedom in this age is characterized most essentially by suffering (Rom 5:3–5), brought about by the knowledge that, here, we will not yet ever experience the righteousness that we already have by promise. But we do have the power to resist sin. That is the shape of our freedom while we wait for the completion of our freedom in the coming of Christ.

Two examples help lay out the practical parameters that Scripture reveals regarding the freedom that a Christian has in Christ. The first example is that of the recovering alcoholic. Like a Christian, who *remains* a sinner even though 100 percent justified, a recovering alcoholic *remains* an alcoholic to the end of his days. The matter of their respective deliverances is also similar. Without exception, every recovering alcoholic came to the realization that deliverance from their lethal, enslaving affliction was terrifyingly no longer possible by any personal effort. A higher power, outside of themselves, was needed. And they bear witness to the reality of the *person* who effected that deliverance, and the continuing effectiveness of that higher power at every AA meeting. So also a Christian.

Lutherans insist that this salutary realization of our need for deliverance results from the terror that our sin is lethal and inescapable—a realization that is effected only by the second use of the Law. Only then do we welcome the fact that our deliverance must be by Christ alone, by the cross alone, by faith alone, by grace alone, and by the word alone. There is definitively no cooperation in our deliverance. Lutherans are just more definitive about the Who and what of the higher power than the recovering alcoholic. Once again, like a recovering alcoholic, Christian freedom from their former slavery consists of never-ending resistance to that indwelling flesh, "one day at a time." Finally, when bearing witness at AA meetings, recovering alcoholics begin, without fail, by first stating their name and then stating, "I am an alcoholic." The analog to this salutary procedure in a Christian church is the personal confession of sin near the beginning of worship. Centuries-old traditional Christian worship examples show that this was never optional. To reinforce the centrality of this deliverance by Christ, the proclamation of the day, itself, was always centered around the forgiveness of sin. Luther insisted, without exception, that this be the core of all evangelical preaching. The absolution from sin by the announcement of the word of God is the power that creates the freedom to live humanly in resistance to the chaos endemic in our current world.

The second example comes from an interview that an American reporter had with a French resistance family after the close of World War II. A family member had been limited in their fight against the Nazi regime to distributing mimeographed fliers to inform others of critical events and possible opportunities for resistance. The interviewer was astonished that in the face of such monolithic tyranny and terror, this person would engage in such a demonstrably puny act of resistance. After all, such an act by itself had no way of creating any measurable effect against the tyranny. Far worse, the penalty of discovery would inevitably lead to the execution of her whole family. She was asked why she nevertheless performed this "useless" act of resistance. She said that calculation of success could not enter her decision because resistance, in any form, *was the only way to stay morally sane.*

Notice that the actions depicted in these two situations have nothing to do with the imagined necessity of the direction of the Law. Instead, they are works that flow from faith alone. They are evidence of Paul's teaching that faith, and not Law, is the only power capable of creating these human behaviors.

Tactics of Resistance to the Power of Death

All the common realities that we encounter every day including illness, pain, abandonment, loneliness, alienation, unemployment, the burdening of the daily work of people with meaninglessness, the astounding waste in the face of appalling human need, the discouraging reality that things and relationships inevitably fall apart—all these are apparitions of death. *There is no other moral reality in the world besides death except the word of God.* And so God enters his Christians into this final contest against the power of death by appointing the power of the Holy Spirit, beginning at Pentecost. The Holy Spirit's indwelling our very bodies continues to make the word of God incarnate in every Christian action.

In Scripture, the Holy Spirit is never used to impress. Rather, the Holy Spirit names God's faithfulness to his creation. The Holy Spirit imprints the word of God needed in each specific situation upon the heart of the believer. The word of God inheres in your very own creation. Therefore, there is no excuse for nonaction. The word of God is at work pervasively, incessantly, and in celebration to renew all creation against the persistent attacks of death. Christians, in every action, are prompted by the expectancy to encounter the Holy Spirit in all events. As Luther writes in the Small Catechism on the Lord's Prayer, God's will is done "when God breaks and hinders every evil counsel and will which would not let us hallow the name of God nor let His kingdom come, such as the will of the devil, the world, and our flesh; but strengthens and keeps us steadfast in His Word and in faith unto our end. This is His gracious and good will."[1]

Each charisma of the Holy Spirit is given to his Christians to engage in this mortal strife and resistance to the power of death. The list of these charismatic gifts in Scripture is extensive. On the positive side they are given to renew creation itself by building up the body of Christ—the church in the world. On the negative side they equip us for mortal combat. The partial list of these gifts of the Spirit are recorded in Rom 12 and in 1 Cor 12. Notably, the first group is listed in the new ethical section of Paul's teaching titled "being transformed by the renewal of your mind" (Rom 12:2). These charisma include, but are not limited to:

- Prophecy
- Service
- Teaching
- Exhortation
- Contribution

1. Luther, "3rd Petition," 11.

- Leading
- Acts of mercy
- Loving one another with brotherly affection
- Patience under persecution
- Blessing those who persecute you
- Living peacefully with all
- Forswearing all vengeance
- Overcoming evil with good
- The utterance of wisdom
- The utterance of knowledge
- Faith
- The working of miracles
- The ability to distinguish between spirits
- Tongues
- The interpretation of tongues

All these serve as acts of resistance that also renew creation and build up the body of Christ. *This life beyond the Law and without the Law is certainly not without shape in Paul's teaching!*

The gift of tongues, the gift of healing, and the gift of exorcism serve as three nonintuitive examples of how each charisma is used by God to defeat the reign of death, here and now. Freed from fantastic views of tongues, one can see concretely how it led radically to increasing the scope of evangelism to the whole world.

> Ecstatic utterance meant the emancipation of human beings from the bonds of nation, culture, race, language, ethnicity. At Pentecost, speaking in tongues is the sublime and notorious worship of God. . . . There were those who misconstrued that extraordinary public and political happening, supposing the people who praised God rather than the Antichrist to be incoherent and drunk and foolish. There are those today who view the phenomenon of tongues in a similar way.[2]

---

2. Stringfellow, *Ethic For Christians*, 147.

In a less political telling, Christians who have this charisma all report the increased intimacy that it brings in their union with the word of God and, with that, a renewed ability to recognize the specific way that God is sending us to serve. A related, recurring example is that some Christians receive "words from the Lord" that they are directed to give to another, words whose context they themselves cannot understand, but which, when they are delivered, are known instantly and comfortably by those to whom God sends them. God has provided this for me at least twice, both significantly.

Consider next the Holy Spirit's charisma of healing as an act of resistance. "In raising Lazarus, Jesus reveals what is implicit, but hidden, in all of the healing episodes, that is, his authority over death, his conclusive power over death, his triumph over death, and all the death can do, and all the death means."[3] When congregations include healing services in the midst of worship, few see this as a witness of Jesus's triumph against the power of death. But it is. It is our witness that the power of death is coming to an end. Such an act of resistance also forms part of our current witness to the imminent return of Jesus to complete the coming of life eternal.

Additionally, when we are engaged in the prayer for healing, we are immediately made aware that we are helpless to effect the outcome of our request, but are entirely leaning upon the power that resides outside of us. We are emphatically not engaged in a cooperative process. Here again, the truth, Christ alone, is impressed upon us.

The third instance of resistance where Christians yield no tribute to the power of death is through the charisma of exorcism. Current baptismal services have retained only a small instance of exorcism, which was once a major component part of this sacrament. The only part left is the question, "Do you renounce the devil and all his works and ways?" At which point, in orthodox churches, the sponsors at one time turned away and spat in contempt upon the floor. Holy baptism makes it clear from the very start that we are, in our baptism, enlisted in mortal and unceasing warfare against sin, death, and the power of the devil. The Lord's Prayer also contains a daily exorcism: "Deliver us from the evil one." These two more liturgical examples reveal that the nature of the resistant combat is daily, even moment by moment. This is how a Christian stays sane. Exorcism has become more necessary in our current life where such actual evil, spiritual possession of people's bodies has become

---

3. Stringfellow, *Ethic For Christians*, 149.

more common. Thus this charisma is no longer ancillary. Such bondage as spiritual possession simply does not yield to modern medical models that are limited to somatic or psychological therapies. In his book *The People of the Lie*, a trained physician, M. Scott Peck, described the practice and necessity of such resistance. Again, when entering into combat with a spiritual personality who knows your sins and weaknesses better than you, yourself, the exorcist feels bare naked. Entering this combat without the knowledge that one stands only by the authority and covering of the Holy Spirit is madness. Christ alone is our refuge and strength, a very present help in trouble (Ps 46).

Living Humanly in Death's Country

So how do we live humanly to celebrate life in the midst of death's reign? First, Christians have been given charisma to discern that in every event, whatsoever, there occurs *together*:

- the moral reality of the *power of death*, but which is now forever resisted at the same time with the incarnation of the *word of God*;
- the *demonic* and the dehumanizing, but which are now resisted in every instance by the *power of the resurrection*;
- the *portents of the awful Apocalypse*, but which are now recognized without fear because of the accompanying signs of the *imminence of Jesus's return*. (C. S. Lewis nobly captures this expectation for children in his work *The Lion, the Witch and the Wardrobe*.)

Biblical living is sacramental in that is hangs upon a bare word of God and nothing else. It is certainly not moralistic or pietistic or religious. Biblical living is watchful for the consummation of the promise, but does not strive to undo the power of death, because we know that the power of death has already been undone. Biblical living is being marinated day by day in the word of God, which alone delivers us from despair over the very evident continuation of sin in our flesh. Biblical living originates in this consolation that Paul names everywhere in 2 Corinthians. The audacity of Christians in their present situation to courageously utter "no" to sin is the signal of a lively hope, a hope transcending the power of death. Our hope may not yet be visible, but our resistance signals that it is certain.

Christ the Lord reigns already! Because this is so, in Gal 6, Paul urges all Christians to take up the whole armor of God that we might be able to stand, spiritually, against what only Christians discern as the spiritual powers. It is the Holy Spirit who helps us recognize the unseen malignant powers behind the visible events. Peace on earth is not a sentimental adage. It was the angels' (*stratia*, meaning "soldiers"[4]) proclamation that announces that Jesus's first coming in his incarnation and birth at Bethlehem (see Luke 2:13–14) was the beginning of the end in God's final warfare against these tyrannical powers. Peace on earth also announces the nearing approach of a second coming where these powers will experience their final judgment under the Lordship of Jesus Christ. When Christian martyrs go down to defeat, their resistance to the power of death, to the very end of their lives, their courage is the most portentous proclamation to the powers of darkness that their time of judgment is drawing ever closer. We have the assurance that in the coming of Jesus the rulers and the powers of this age will be judged. This judgment does mean the destruction of these powers. So, hearing the promise of the word of God, Christian rejoicing is constant, the anticipation is eager, and faith is steady that the expectation is imminent.

To summarize succinctly, the shape of Christian freedom is, moment by moment, resistance to the power of death, using only the power of the word of God. I cannot say it better than William Stringfellow, who wrote, "This foolishness of the saints . . . is wrought in the relationship of justification and judgment, in which one who knows justification to be a gift of God, is spared no aggression of the power of death, but concedes no tribute to the power of death, while awaiting the vindication of the Word of God in the coming of Jesus Christ in judgment."[5]

---

4. BAGD, s.v. "στρατιά."
5. Stringfellow, *Conscience & Obedience*, 112.

Appendix I

Solid Declaration Article VI. The Third Use of the Law[1]

¹ Since the Law of God is useful, 1. not only to the end that external discipline and decency are maintained by it against wild, disobedient men; 2. likewise, that through it men are brought to a knowledge of their sins; 3. but also that, when they have been born anew by the Spirit of God, converted to the Lord, and thus the veil of Moses has been lifted from them, they live and walk in the Law, a dissension has occurred between some few theologians concerning this third and last use of the Law.

² For the one side taught and maintained that the regenerate do not learn the new obedience, or in what good works they ought to walk, from the Law, and that this teaching [concerning good works] is not to be urged thence [from the Law], because they have been made free by the Son of God, have become the temples of His Spirit, and therefore do freely of themselves what God requires of them, by the prompting and impulse of the Holy Ghost, just as the sun of itself, without any [foreign] impulse, completes its ordinary course.

³ Over against this the other side taught: Although the truly believing are verily moved by God's Spirit, and thus, according to the inner man, do God's will from a free spirit, yet it is just the Holy Ghost who uses the written Law for instruction with them, by which the truly believing also learn to serve God, not according to their own thoughts, but according to His written Law and Word, which is a sure rule and standard of a godly life and walk, how to order it in accordance with the eternal and immutable will of God.

⁴ For the explanation and final settlement of this dissent we unanimously believe, teach, and confess that although the truly believing and

---

1. Tappert, *Book of Concord*, 563–68.

truly converted to God and justified Christians are liberated and made free from the curse of the Law, yet they should daily exercise themselves in the Law of the Lord, as it is written, Ps. 1:2;119:1: Blessed is the man whose delight is in the Law of the Lord, and in His Law doth he meditate day and night. For the Law is a mirror in which the will of God, and what pleases Him, are exactly portrayed, and which should [therefore] be constantly held up to the believers and be diligently urged upon them without ceasing.

⁵ For although the Law is not made for a righteous man, as the apostle testifies 1 Tim. 1:9, but for the unrighteous, yet this is not to be understood in the bare meaning, that the justified are to live without Law. For the Law of God has been written in their heart, and also to the first man immediately after his creation a Law was given according to which he was to conduct himself. But the meaning of St. Paul is that the Law cannot burden with its curse those who have been reconciled to God through Christ; nor must it vex the regenerate with its coercion, because they have pleasure in God's Law after the inner man.

⁶ And, indeed, if the believing and elect children of God were completely renewed in this life by the indwelling Spirit, so that in their nature and all its powers they were entirely free from sin, they would need no Law, and hence no one to drive them either, but they would do of themselves, and altogether voluntarily, without any instruction, admonition, urging or driving of the Law, what they are in duty bound to do according to God's will; just as the sun, the moon, and all the constellations of heaven have their regular course of themselves, unobstructed, without admonition, urging, driving, force, or compulsion, according to the order of God which God once appointed for them, yea, just as the holy angels render an entirely voluntary obedience.

⁷ However, believers are not renewed in this life perfectly or completely, completive vel consummative [as the ancients say]; for although their sin is covered by the perfect obedience of Christ, so that it is not imputed to believers for condemnation, and also the mortification of the old Adam and the renewal in the spirit of their mind is begun through the Holy Ghost, nevertheless the old Adam clings to them still in their nature and all its internal and external powers.

⁸ Of this the apostle has written Rom. 7:18ff.: I know that in me [that is, in my flesh] dwelleth no good thing. And again: For that which I do I allow not; for what I would, that do I not; but what I hate, that I do; Likewise: I see another Law in my members, warring against the Law

of my mind, and bringing me into captivity to the Law of sin. Likewise, Gal. 5:17: The flesh lusteth against the spirit and the spirit against the flesh; and these are contrary the one to the other, so that ye cannot do the things that ye would.

⁹ Therefore, because of these lusts of the flesh the truly believing, elect, and regenerate children of God need in this life not only the daily instruction and admonition, warning, and threatening of the Law, but also frequently punishments, that they may be roused [the old man is driven out of them] and follow the Spirit of God, as it is written Ps. 119:71: It is good for me that I have been afflicted, that I might learn Thy statutes. And again, 1 Cor. 9:27: I keep under my body and bring it into subjection, lest that, by any means, when I have preached to others, I myself should be a castaway. And again, Heb. 12:8: But if ye be without chastisement, whereof all are partakers, then are ye bastards and not sons; as Dr. Luther has fully explained this at greater length in the Summer Part of the Church Postil, on the Epistle for the Nineteenth Sunday after Trinity.

¹⁰ But we must also explain distinctively what the Gospel does, produces, and works towards the new obedience of believers, and what is the office of the Law in this matter, as regards the good works of believers.

¹¹ For the Law says indeed that it is God's will and command that we should walk in a new life, but it does not give the power and ability to begin and do it; but the Holy Ghost, who is given and received, not through the Law, but through the preaching of the Gospel, Gal. 3:14, renews the heart.

¹² Thereafter the Holy Ghost employs the Law so as to teach the regenerate from it, and to point out and show them in the Ten Commandments what is the [good and] acceptable will of God, Rom. 12:2, in what good works God hath before ordained that they should walk, Eph. 2:10. He exhorts them thereto, and when they are idle, negligent, and rebellious in this matter because of the flesh, He reproves them on that account through the Law, so that He carries on both offices together: He slays and makes alive; He leads into hell and brings up again. For His office is not only to comfort, but also to reprove, as it is written: When the Holy Ghost is come, He will reprove the world (which includes also the old Adam) of sin, and of righteousness, and of judgment.

¹³ But sin is everything that is contrary to God's Law.

¹⁴ And St. Paul says: All Scripture given by inspiration of God is profitable for doctrine, for reproof, etc., and to reprove is the peculiar office of the Law. Therefore, as often as believers stumble, they are reproved

by the Holy Spirit from the Law, and by the same Spirit are raised up and comforted again with the preaching of the Holy Gospel.

15 But in order that, as far as possible, all misunderstanding may be prevented, and the distinction between the works of the Law and those of the Spirit be properly taught and preserved it is to be noted with especial diligence that when we speak of good works which are in accordance with God's Law (for otherwise they are not good works), then the word Law has only one sense, namely, the immutable will of God, according to which men are to conduct themselves in their lives.

16 The difference, however, is in the works, because of the difference in the men who strive to live according to this Law and will of God. For as long as man is not regenerate, and [therefore] conducts himself according to the Law and does the works because they are commanded thus, from fear of punishment or desire for reward, he is still under the Law, and his works are called by St. Paul properly works of the Law, for they are extorted by the Law, as those of slaves; and these are saints after the order of Cain [that is, hypocrites].

17 But when man is born anew by the Spirit of God, and liberated from the Law, that is, freed from this driver, and is led by the Spirit of Christ, he lives according to the immutable will of God comprised in the Law, and so far as he is born anew, does everything from a free, cheerful spirit; and these are called not properly works of the Law, but works and fruits of the Spirit, or as St. Paul names it, the Law of the mind and the Law of Christ. For such men are no more under the Law, but under grace, as St. Paul says, Rom. 8:2 [Rom. 7:23; 1 Cor. 9:21].

18 But since believers are not completely renewed in this world, but the old Adam clings to them even to the grave, there also remains in them the struggle between the spirit and the flesh. Therefore they delight indeed in God's Law according to the inner man, but the Law in their members struggles against the Law in their mind; hence they are never without the Law, and nevertheless are not under, but in the Law, and live and walk in the Law of the Lord, and yet do nothing from constraint of the Law.

19 But as far as the old Adam is concerned, which still clings to them, he must be driven not only with the Law, but also with punishments; nevertheless he does everything against his will and under coercion, no less than the godless are driven and held in obedience by the threats of the Law, 1 Cor. 9:27; Rom. 7:18. 19.

20 So, too, this doctrine of the Law is needful for believers, in order that they may not hit upon a holiness and devotion of their own, and under the pretext of the Spirit of God set up a self-chosen worship, without God's Word and command, as it is written Deut. 12:8,28,32: Ye shall not do . . . every man whatsoever is right in his own eyes, etc., but observe and hear all these words which I command thee. Thou shalt not add thereto, nor diminish therefrom.

21 So, too, the doctrine of the Law, in and with [the exercise of] the good works of believers, is necessary for the reason that otherwise man can easily imagine that his work and life are entirely pure and perfect. But the Law of God prescribes to believers good works in this way, that it shows and indicates at the same time, as in a mirror, that in this life they are still imperfect and impure in us, so that we must say with the beloved Paul, 1 Cor. 4:4: I know nothing by myself; yet am I not hereby justified. Thus Paul, when exhorting the regenerate to good works, presents to them expressly the Ten Commandments, Rom. 13:9; and that his good works are imperfect and impure he recognizes from the Law, Rom. 7:7ff; and David declares Ps. 119:32: Viam mandatorum tuorum cucurri, I will run the way of Thy commandments; but enter not into judgment with Thy servant, for in Thy sight shall no man living be justified, Ps. 143:2.

22 But how and why the good works of believers, although in this life they are imperfect and impure because of sin in the flesh, are nevertheless acceptable and well-pleasing to God, is not taught by the Law, which requires an altogether perfect, pure obedience if it is to please God. But the Gospel teaches that our spiritual offerings are acceptable to God through faith for Christ's sake, 1 Pet. 2:5; Heb. 11:4ff.

23 In this way Christians are not under the Law, but under grace, because by faith in Christ the persons are freed from the curse and condemnation of the Law; and because their good works, although they are still imperfect and impure, are acceptable to God through Christ; moreover, because so far as they have been born anew according to the inner man, they do what is pleasing to God, not by coercion of the Law, but by the renewing of the Holy Ghost, voluntarily and spontaneously from their hearts; however, they maintain nevertheless a constant struggle against the old Adam.

24 For the old Adam, as an intractable, refractory ass, is still a part of them, which must be coerced to the obedience of Christ, not only by the teaching, admonition, force and threatening of the Law, but also oftentimes by the club of punishments and troubles, until the body of

sin is entirely put off, and man is perfectly renewed in the resurrection, when he will need neither the preaching of the Law nor its threatenings and punishments, as also the Gospel any longer; for these belong to this [mortal and] imperfect life.

[25] But as they will behold God face to face, so they will, through the power of the indwelling Spirit of God, do the will of God [the heavenly Father] with unmingled joy, voluntarily, unconstrained, without any hindrance, with entire purity and perfection, and will rejoice in it eternally.

[26] Accordingly, we reject and condemn as an error pernicious and detrimental to Christian discipline, as also to true godliness, the teaching that the Law, in the above-mentioned way and degree, should not be urged upon Christians and the true believers, but only upon the unbelieving, unchristians, and impenitent.

Appendix II

The Heidelberg Disputation
The New Reformation Theology in Twenty-Eight Articles

The Problem of Good Works: Theses 1–12[1]

1) The Law of God, the most salutary doctrine of life, cannot advance humans on their way to righteousness, but rather hinders them.

2) Much less can human works, which are done over and over again with the aid of natural precepts, so to speak, lead to that end.

3) Although the works of man always seem attractive and good, they are nevertheless likely to be mortal sins.

4) Although the works of God are always unattractive and appear evil, they are nevertheless really eternal merits.

5) The works of men are thus not mortal sins (we speak of works that are apparently good), as though they were crimes.

6) The works of God (we speak of those that He does through man) are thus not merits, as though they were sinless.

7) The works of the righteous would be mortal sins if they would not be feared as mortal sins by the righteous themselves out of pious fear of God.

8) By so much more are the works of man mortal sins when they are done without fear and in unadulterated evil self-security.

9) To say that works without Christ are dead, but not mortal, appears to constitute a perilous surrender of the fear of God.

---

1. Section titles are from Forde, *On Being a Theologian*.

10) Indeed, it is very difficult to see how a work can be dead and at the same time not a harmful and mortal sin.

11) Arrogance cannot be avoided, or true hope be present, unless the judgment of condemnation is feared in every work.

12) In the sight of God, sins are then truly venial when they are feared by men to be mortal.

The Problem of the Will: Theses 13–18

13) Free will, after the fall, exists in name only, and as long as it does what it is able to do, it commits a mortal sin.

14) Free will, after the fall, has power to do good only in a passive capacity, but it can always do evil in an active capacity.

15) Nor could free will remain in a state of innocence, much less do good, in an active capacity, but only in its passive capacity.

16) The person who believes that he can obtain grace by doing what is in him, adds sin to sin, so that he becomes doubly guilty.

17) Nor does speaking in this manner give cause for despair, but for arousing the desire to humble oneself and seek the grace of Christ.

18) It is certain that man must utterly despair of his own ability before he is prepared to receive the grace of Christ.

The Great Divide—The Way of Glory vs. the Way of the Cross, or, "How Does One Know God?"

Theses 19–24

19) That person does not deserve to be called a theologian who claims to see into the invisible things of God.

20) But that person deserves to be called a theologian who comprehends what is visible of God through suffering and the cross.

21) The theologian of glory calls evil good, and good evil. The theologian of the cross says what a thing is.

22) That wisdom which perceives the invisible things of God by thinking in terms of works, completely puffs up, blinds, and hardens.

23) The Law works the wrath of God, kills, curses, accuses, judges, and damns everything that is not in Christ. (the Law is never your friend!)

24) Yet, that wisdom is not of itself evil, nor is the Law to be evaded; but without the theology of the cross man misuses the best in the worst manner.

God's Work in Us: The Righteousness of Faith; Theses 25–28

25) He is not righteous who works much, but he who, without work, believes much in Christ.

26) The Law says, "do this," and it is never done. Grace says, "believe this," and everything is already done.

27) Rightly speaking, therefore, the work of Christ should be called the operative power, and our work the operation; so our operation is pleasing to God by the grace of the operative power. (Here one requires a robust conception of the role of the Holy Spirit)

28) The love of God does not first discover, but creates, what is pleasing to it. The love of man comes into being through attraction to what pleases it.

Bibliography

Augustine. *On Nature and Grace*. Translated by Peter Holmes and Robert Ernest Wallis, revised by Benjamin B. Warfield. Vol. 5, Nicene and Post-Nicene Fathers, Series 1, edited by Philip Schaff. Buffalo: Christian Literature, 1887. Revised for New Advent by Kevin Knight. https://www.newadvent.org/fathers/1503.htm.

Aung San Suu Kyi. *Freedom from Fear and Other Writings*. Edited by Michael Aris. New York: Penguin, 1991.

Baring-Gould, S. "Onward, Christian Soldiers." Hymnary, 1865. https://hymnary.org/text/onward_christian_soldiers_marching_as.

Beker, J. Christiaan. *Suffering and Hope: The Biblical Vision and the Human Predicament*. Philadelphia: Fortress, 1987.

Durant, Will. *Our Oriental Heritage*. Vol 1, *The Story of Civilization*. New York: Simon and Schuster, 1954.

Ebeling, Gerhard. *Luther: An Introduction to His Thought*. Translated by R. A. Wilson. Philadelphia: Fortress, 1964.

Forde, Gerhard O. *On Being a Theologian of the Cross*. Grand Rapids: Eerdmans, 1997.

———. *Theology Is for Proclamation*. Minneapolis: Augsburg Fortress, 1990.

Hopman, Nicholas. "Luther's *Antinomian Disputations* and *lex aeterna*." *Lutheran Quarterly* 30 (2016) 152–80.

Hugo, Victor. *Les Miserables*. Translated by Christine Donougher. New York: Penguin, 2015.

Iwand, Hans J. *The Righteousness of Faith According to Luther*. Edited by Virgil Thompson, translated by Randi Lundell. Eugene, OR: Wipf & Stock, 2008.

Lewis, C. S. *The Lion, the Witch and the Wardrobe*. London: Bles, 1950.

———. *Surprised by Joy: The Shape of My Early Life*. New York: Harcourt, Brace & World, 1955.

Luther, Martin. "3rd Petition." In "Part III: The Lord's Prayer" of the *Small Catechism* in the *Book of Concord*. https://thebookofconcord.org/small-catechism-part-iii/petition-3/.

Obermann, Heiko A. *Luther: Man Between God and the Devil*. Translated by Eileen Walliser-Schwarzbart. New Have: Yale University Press, 1989.

Peck, M. Scott. *People of the Lie: The Hope for Healing Human Evil*. New York: Simon & Schuster, 1983.

Prenter, Regin. *Spiritus Creator*. Translated by John M. Jensen. Philadelphia: Muhlenberg, 1953.

"Religion." In *Encyclopedia Britannica*. 15th ed. Chicago: 2009.

Scaer, David P. "The Third Use of the Law: Resolving the Tension." *Concordia Theological Quarterly* 69:3–4 (July/October 2005) 237–58. https://ctsfw.net/media/pdfs/scaerthirduseresolvetension.pdf.

Spurgeon, Charles H. *Morning and Evening*. Edited by Alistair Begg. Wheaton, IL: Crossway, 2003.

Stringfellow, William. *Conscience & Obedience: The Politics of Romans 13 and Revelation 13 in Light of the Second Coming*. Waco, TX: Word, 1977.

———. *An Ethic For Christians and Other Aliens in a Strange Land*. Waco, TX: Word, 1973.

Tappert, Theodore, ed. *Book of Concord: The Confessions of the Evangelical Lutheran Church*. Philadelphia: Muhlenberg, 1965.

Wikisource Contributors. "Canons and Decrees of the Council of Trent/SessionVI/Justification." Wikisource, last updated February 21, 2024. https://en.wikisource.org/wiki/Canons_and_Decrees_of_the_Council_of_Trent/Session_VI/Justification.

Wright, N. T. "The Letter to the Romans." In *Acts; Introduction to Epistolary Literature; Romans; 1 Corinthians*, edited by Leander E. Keck et al., 393–770. Vol. 10 of *The New Interpreter's Bible*. Nashville: Abingdon, 2002.

www.ingramcontent.com/pod-product-compliance
Lightning Source LLC
Chambersburg PA
CBHW072151160426
43197CB00012B/2342